FEDERAL BUREAU OF INVESTIGATION
ANNUAL FINANCIAL STATEMENTS
FISCAL YEAR 2015

OFFICE OF THE INSPECTOR GENERAL
COMMENTARY AND SUMMARY

This audit report contains the Annual Financial Statements of the Federal Bureau of Investigation (FBI) for the fiscal years (FY) ended September 30, 2015, and September 30, 2014. Under the direction of the Office of the Inspector General (OIG), Kearney & Company, PC (Kearney & Company) performed the FBI's audit in accordance with auditing standards generally accepted in the United States of America. The FY 2015 audit resulted in an unmodified opinion on the financial statements. An unmodified opinion means that the financial statements are presented fairly, in all material respects, in accordance with U.S. generally accepted accounting principles. The FY 2014 financial statement audit was performed by KPMG LLP and resulted in an unmodified opinion (OIG Audit Report No. 15-06).

Kearney & Company also issued reports on internal control over financial reporting and on compliance and other matters. The auditors did not identify any material weaknesses, nor did they report any significant deficiencies in the FY 2015 *Independent Auditor's Report on Internal Control over Financial Reporting Based on an Audit of Financial Statements Performed in Accordance with Government Auditing Standards*. No instances of non-compliance or other matters were identified during the audit that are required to be reported under *Government Auditing Standards*, in the FY 2015 *Independent Auditor's Report on Compliance and Other Matters Based on an Audit of Financial Statements Performed in Accordance with Government Auditing Standards*. Additionally, Kearney & Company's tests disclosed no instances in which the FBI's financial management systems did not comply substantially with the *Federal Financial Management Improvement Act of 1996*.

The OIG reviewed Kearney & Company's reports and related documentation and made necessary inquiries of its representatives. Our review, as differentiated from an audit in accordance with *Government Auditing Standards*, was not intended to enable us to express, and we do not express, an opinion on the FBI's financial statements, conclusions about the effectiveness of internal control, conclusions on whether the FBI's financial management systems complied substantially with the *Federal Financial Management Improvement Act of 1996*, or conclusions on compliance and other matters. Kearney & Company is responsible for the attached auditors' reports dated November 4, 2015, and the conclusions expressed in the reports. However, our review disclosed no instances where Kearney & Company did not comply, in all material respects, with auditing standards generally accepted in the United States of America.

This page intentionally left blank.

AUDIT OF THE
FEDERAL BUREAU OF INVESTIGATION
ANNUAL FINANCIAL STATEMENTS
FISCAL YEAR 2015

TABLE OF CONTENTS

This page intentionally left blank.

U.S. DEPARTMENT OF JUSTICE

FEDERAL BUREAU OF INVESTIGATION

MANAGEMENT'S DISCUSSION AND ANALYSIS (UNAUDITED)

This page intentionally left blank.

U.S. DEPARTMENT OF JUSTICE
FEDERAL BUREAU OF INVESTIGATION
MANAGEMENT'S DISCUSSION AND ANALYSIS
(UNAUDITED)

MISSION

The Federal Bureau of Investigation (FBI or Bureau) is a component of the United States (U.S.) Department of Justice (DOJ or the Department) and a member of the U.S. Intelligence Community (IC). The mission of the FBI is to protect and defend the U.S. against terrorist and foreign intelligence threats, to uphold and enforce the criminal laws of the U.S., and to provide leadership and criminal justice services to federal, state, municipal, and international agencies and partners.

The FBI priorities guide how the FBI addresses its wide range of responsibilities. In executing the following priorities, the FBI produces and uses intelligence to protect the nation from threats and to bring justice to those who violate the law. The first eight priorities are listed in order of precedence. The final two are all-encompassing functions that support the Bureau's mission and objectives. The ten priorities are:

1. Protect the U.S. from terrorist attack;
2. Protect the U.S. against foreign intelligence operations and espionage;
3. Protect the U.S. against cyber-based attacks and high-technology crimes;
4. Combat public corruption at all levels;
5. Protect civil rights;
6. Combat transnational and national criminal organizations and enterprises;
7. Combat major white-collar crime;
8. Combat significant violent crime;
9. Support federal, state, local, and international partners; and
10. Upgrade technology to successfully perform the FBI's mission.

The methodology by which the FBI allocates gross costs and earned revenue across its three Strategic Goals (SGs or Goals) is consistent with the methodology used to allocate the FBI's budget to the three SGs in the Fiscal Year (FY) 2016 Authorization and Budget Request to Congress. The three SGs are:

Goal 1: Prevent Terrorism and Promote the Nation's Security Consistent with the Rule of Law;

Goal 2: Prevent Crime, Protect the Rights of the American People, and Enforce Federal Law; and

Goal 3: Ensure and Support the Fair, Impartial, Efficient, and Transparent Administration of Justice at the Federal, State, Local, Tribal, and International Levels.

Priorities 1 through 3 support Goal 1, priorities 3 through 8 support Goal 2, and priorities 9 and 10 support all three Goals.

ORGANIZATION STRUCTURE

Along with the FBI's headquarters (HQ or Headquarters) located in Washington, D.C., the FBI operates 56 field offices and approximately 360 resident agencies across the U.S. and its territories. The FBI also operates more than 64 Legal Attaché (Legat) offices and more than 20 sub-offices in over 70 foreign countries.

The Criminal Justice Information Services Division (CJIS), including the new Biometrics Technology Center, is located in Clarksburg, West Virginia. The Laboratory Division, Operational Technology Division (Engineering Research Facility), Training Division, and Critical Incident Response Group are located in Quantico, Virginia. Other major FBI facilities include the Hazardous Devices School and the Terrorist Explosive Device Analytical Center at Redstone Arsenal in Huntsville, Alabama. Other specialized facilities, such as the Regional Computer Forensic Laboratories, are located at various locations across the country.

FBI HQ provides centralized operational, policy, and administrative support to investigations and programs conducted throughout the U.S. and in foreign countries. Under the direction of the FBI Director and Deputy Director, the HQ functions are organized among five branches headed by Executive Assistant Directors and several supporting divisions managed by the Associate Deputy Director. Each field office is overseen by a Special Agent in Charge or an Assistant Director in Charge. Resident agencies are managed by Supervisory Special Agents.

In FY 2015, the FBI's appropriated staffing level consisted of 13,074 Special Agents, 3,064 Intelligence Analysts, and 18,899 professional staff along with an additional 3,042 reimbursable positions.

FINANCIAL STRUCTURE

For purposes of executing its budget, the FBI's funds are organized into the following categories: appropriated single year, multi-year, and no-year Salaries and Expense funds and appropriated no-year Construction funds. These funds include new appropriations, transfers of appropriations from other federal agencies, and the carry-over of prior years' unobligated balances for multi-year and no-year appropriated funds. The FBI also receives reimbursable funding from other agencies for services rendered.

FY 2015 RESOURCE INFORMATION

Table 1 presents the sources of financing for FBI resources distinguished by Earned Revenue, Budgetary Financing Sources, and Other Financing Sources. Table 2 describes how the FBI spent its resources, divided across Strategic Goals 1, 2, and 3.

Table 1. Source of FBI Resources
(Dollars in Thousands)

Source	FY 2015	FY 2014	Change%
Earned Revenue	$ 1,163,741	$ 1,108,282	5%
Budgetary Financing Sources			
Appropriations Received	8,436,569	8,343,284	1%
Appropriation Transferred-In/Out	(35,187)	(34,706)	(1%)
Nonexchange Revenue	21	29	(28%)
Transfers-In/Out Without Reimbursement	548,515	(1,651)	33,323%
Other Adjustments and Other Budgetary Financing Sources	-	-	n/m
Other Financing Sources			
Donations and Forfeitures of Property	-	-	n/m
Transfers-In/Out Without Reimbursement	25,800	112,458	(77%)
Imputed Financing from Costs Absorbed by Others	257,696	294,644	(13%)
Other Financing Sources	(10,836)	(8,193)	(32%)
Total	**$ 10,386,319**	**$ 9,814,147**	**6%**

Table 2. How FBI Resources are Spent
(Dollars in Thousands)

Strategic Goal (SG)	FY 2015	FY 2014	Change%
SG 1: Prevent Terrorism and Promote the Nation's Security Consistent with the Rule of Law			
Gross Cost	$ 5,310,342	$ 5,091,986	
Less: Earned Revenue	274,532	310,145	
Net Cost	$ 5,035,810	$ 4,781,841	5%
SG 2: Prevent Crime, Protect the Rights of the American People, and Enforce Federal Law			
Gross Cost	$ 3,555,518	$ 3,047,534	
Less: Earned Revenue	306,527	302,436	
Net Cost	$ 3,248,991	$ 2,745,098	18%
SG 3: Ensure and Support the Fair, Impartial, Efficient, and Transparent Administration of Justice at the Federal, State, Local, Tribal, and International Levels			
Gross Cost	$ 960,334	$ 918,839	
	582,682	495,701	
Net Cost	$ 377,652	$ 423,138	(11%)
Total Gross Cost	**$ 9,826,194**	**$ 9,058,359**	
Less: Total Earned Revenue	**1,163,741**	**1,108,282**	
Total Net Cost of Operations	**$ 8,662,453**	**$ 7,950,077**	**9%**

ANALYSIS OF FINANCIAL STATEMENTS

The FBI's financial statements received unmodified audit opinions for FYs 2015 and 2014. These financial statements were prepared from the accounting records of the FBI in conformity with U.S. generally accepted accounting principles issued by the Federal Accounting Standards Advisory Board and presentation guidelines in the Office of Management and Budget (OMB) Circular A-136, *Financial Reporting Requirements.*

Assets: Total Assets was $7.6 billion as of September 30, 2015, an increase of $713 million, or 10 percent, from the previous fiscal year's Total Assets of $6.8 billion. This increase is primarily related to increases in Fund Balance with Treasury (FBwT) and Advances and Prepayments. FBwT increased in FY 2015 by $792 million, or 23 percent, which is primarily due to an increase in appropriated funding. Advances and Prepayments increased in FY 2015 by $65 million, or 550%, which is primarily due to an increase in prepayments to the public in the amount of $40 million in the fourth quarter of FY 2015.

Liabilities: Total Liabilities was $1.4 billion as of September 30, 2015, an increase of $153 million, or 12 percent, from the previous fiscal year's Total Liabilities of $1.2 billion. This increase is primarily due to increases in Accounts Payable with the Public and Other Intragovernmental Liabilities. Accounts Payable with the Public increased by $143 million or 48 percent, offset by a decrease in Intragovernmental Accounts Payable of $47 million, or 27 percent. The increase related to Accounts Payable with the Public is attributed to an increase in open obligations, an increase in recordings related to Work-in-Process (WIP) and timing differences in recognizing Treasury disbursement schedules. Other Intragovernmental Liabilities increased $33 million, or 36 percent, due to increases in Advances from Others and Employer Contributions and Payroll Taxes Payable. Advances from Others increased $25 million driven by an increase in reimbursable agreements with other agencies. Employer Contributions and Payroll Taxes Payable increased $7 million due to a one day increase in the number of days included in the payroll accrual, as compared to FY 2014.

Net Position: Total Net Position was $6.2 billion as of September 30, 2015, an increase of $560 million, or 10 percent, from the previous fiscal year's Total Net Position of $5.6 billion. The increase is primarily due to an increase in Budgetary Financing Sources Transfers-In/Out Without Reimbursement of $550 million, or 33,323 percent. FBI received a Transfer-In of Spectrum Advance Wireless Services (AWS) funding in the amount of $553 million to assume responsibility for radio management for all of DOJ. The increase was offset by a Transfer-Out of $4.8 million of User Fee funding to the Working Capital Fund (WCF).

Net Cost of Operations: Total Net Cost of Operations was $8.7 billion for FY 2015, an increase of $712 million, or nine percent, from Total Net Cost of Operations of $8.0 billion for FY 2014. The increase is primarily attributed to an increase in Gross Costs caused by an investment in criminal and cyber programs across various divisions.

Budgetary Resources: Total Budgetary Resources was $11.7 billion for FY 2015, an increase of $894 million, or eight percent, from Total Budgetary Resources of $10.8 billion in FY 2014. The change is related to increases in Unobligated Balances, Brought Forward on October 1, 2015 of $197 million, Recovery of Prior Year Unpaid Obligations of $28 million, and Appropriations of $644 million.

FY 2015 Financial Highlights

Performance measures included in previous FBI Management's Discussion and Analysis (MD&A) documents may have changed as a result of new information that was unavailable prior to submitting previous financial reports. Due to the requirement to disclose performance data in the MD&A before the close of the data entry period, reports of certain FY 2015 performance measures should be considered tentative and are annotated accordingly. Other subsequent changes to prior year data may have occurred due to factors beyond the control of the FBI's data collection systems (e.g., convictions overturned on appeal). For previously estimated measures, the FBI reviewed and revised certain FY 2014 performance data from the FY 2014 MD&A. The FBI's FY 2016 Authorization and Budget Request to Congress documented these revisions. For FY 2015 MD&A performance estimates, the final results will be reflected in the FY 2017 President's Budget.

Strategic Goal 1, Prevent Terrorism and Promote the Nation's Security Consistent with the Rule of Law, includes the FBI's counterterrorism (CT) and counterintelligence (CI) investigations, intelligence collection and analysis, computer intrusions investigations, and the Weapons of Mass Destruction (WMD) program. In FY 2015, Goal 1 Net Cost was $5.0 billion, a net increase of five percent from FY 2014.

Strategic Goal 2, Prevent Crime, Protect the Rights of the American People, and Enforce Federal Law, includes the majority of the FBI's criminal investigative programs and programs supporting state and local law enforcement. Investigations under Goal 2 includes: organized crime, drugs, violent crime, white-collar crime, and cyber crime. In FY 2015, Goal 2 Net Cost was $3.2 billion, a net increase of 18 percent from FY 2014. The increase is primarily attributed to significant one time nonpersonnel investments. This investment supported the FBI's criminal program, cyber, operational technology and IT infrastructure. The FBI also invested significant resources to hiring in FY 2015 which related to both Goals 1 and 2.

Strategic Goal 3, Ensure and Support the Fair, Impartial, Efficient, and Transparent Administration of Justice at the Federal, State, Local, Tribal, and International Levels, includes the FBI's Integrated Automation Fingerprint Identification Systems, Next Generation Identification, the National Instant Criminal Background Check System, the Law Enforcement National Data Exchange, and other criminal justice services that the FBI offers to law enforcement agencies and local communities. In FY 2015, Goal 3 Net Cost was $0.4 billion, a net decrease of 11 percent from FY 2014. In FY 2015, revenues for Goal 3 increased at a higher rate than costs due to User Fee programs revenue being allocated 100 percent to Goal 3. In FY 2014, User Fee programs revenue were allocated across all three goals. For FY 2015, the result was an overall decrease in Net Cost for Goal 3.

FY 2015 REPORT ON SELECTED RESULTS

STRATEGIC GOAL 1: **Prevent Terrorism and Promote the Nation's Security Consistent with the Rule of Law** *58 percent of the FBI's Net Cost supports this Goal.*

PROGRAM: Counterterrorism

Background/Program Objectives: The FBI is committed to disrupting and preventing terrorism, from thwarting those intending to conduct a terrorist act to investigating financiers of terrorist operations. All CT investigations are managed at Headquarters by the Counterterrorism Division (CTD). CTD provides a centralized, comprehensive, and intelligence-driven approach to addressing both international and domestic terrorism-related matters.

Performance Measure: Number of Terrorism Disruptions

> *FY 2014 Actual Performance:* 214
>
> *FY 2015 Target:* 125
>
> *FY 2015 Actual Performance:* 440

Discussion of FY 2015 Results:

The FBI exceeded its annual target for the number of terrorism disruptions effected through CT investigations. The FBI is committed to stopping terrorism of any kind at any stage as evidenced by its transformation into a proactive agency. To fulfill DOJ's mission of defeating terrorism, the FBI focuses resources on targeting and disrupting terrorist threats and groups by leveraging its workforce and ensuring the use of the latest technology to thwart emerging trends.

Maintaining the proficiency levels of CT agents and Task Force Officers (TFO) is critical to an effective workforce. In FY 2015, 148 TFOs completed the Joint Terrorism Operations Course and 225 CT Career Path Special Agents completed specialized training sponsored by the FBI CTD.

The Guardian Threat Tracking System, a platform used to receive, assess, disseminate and memorialize threats and suspicious activities, has proven to be an important tool for CT investigations. FBI shares information with law enforcement partner agencies, some of which are state-run Fusion Centers, and individual users. Use of the system continued to grow in FY 2015 by both the FBI and Law Enforcement partners, which resulted in an increased exchange between the FBI and Law Enforcement partners.

PROGRAM: Counterintelligence

Background/Program Objectives: Foreign espionage strikes at the heart of U.S. national security, impacting political, military, and economic arenas. The foreign intelligence threat to the U.S. is expanding, becoming more complex and less predictable. While traditional threats to national defense, military operations and policy, intelligence, and science and technology remain, many intelligence threats are expanding their targets to include the burgeoning population of cleared defense contractors. Other sectors affecting U.S. security, most notably sensitive economic information and emerging proprietary technology, are also threatened. Concurrently, foreign threats now have sophisticated networks of governmental and non-governmental entities using a wide array of intelligence collection platforms and engaging in long-term efforts to obtain sensitive information and threaten the security of the U.S.

To facilitate its counterespionage mission, the FBI focuses resources on protecting the nation from foreign espionage attempts by leveraging the Strategic Partnership Coordination (SPC) Program and targeting the highest priority threats as determined by the National Intelligence Priorities Framework (NIPF). The intent of the following measure is to evaluate the impact of CI outreach initiatives against the FBI's counterespionage strategic objectives.

Performance Measure: Percentage of Counterespionage Actions and Disruptions against National Counterintelligence Priorities that Result from FBI Outreach

    FY 2014 Actual Performance: 7.3%

    FY 2015 Target: 10%

    FY 2015 Actual Performance: 14.16%

Discussion of FY 2015 Results:

In FY 2015, espionage remained one of the CI program's most significant threats. In addition to traditional tradecraft used to access economic, national security, and proprietary information, the FBI continued to disrupt and monitor more advanced methods to infiltrate organizations. Of the CI program's total law enforcement actions and disruption activities, espionage-related threats accounted for more than 31 percent of the FBI's total CI accomplishments against NIPF-sponsored actors or entities. These accomplishments included approximately 27 arrests, 12 convictions, and nearly 19 indictments.

The FBI relies heavily on its coordination with the U.S. IC, other government agencies, international partners, and public as well as private entities. These relationships increase intelligence collection, identify emerging threats, and disrupt priority threats. As a result of the SPC Program, the FBI organized regular CI working group meetings, formed alliances with the academic and business sectors, and conducted thousands of briefings to organizations vulnerable to foreign intelligence intrusions. These programs led to more than 6,800 threat briefings, CI awareness presentations, and intelligence disseminations and the establishment of more than 1,359 tripwires (processes established to provide indicators of an emerging threat).

The CI SPC Program demonstrated significant progress toward converting its outreach into productive foreign intelligence collection and investigations. Strategic partnerships contributed to the dissemination of approximately 1,275 finished intelligence products and 337 case openings. As hostile foreign intelligence services use more sophisticated techniques to breach key economic, national security, and technology sectors, it is essential that the FBI develop more robust partnerships outside the intelligence and law enforcement communities. In FY 2016, threat-prioritized strategic outreach will remain an important initiative for the CI program. Further, the CI program will address the emerging threat of foreign nation states increasingly using commercial enterprises to achieve their desired intelligence collection and operational capabilities.

PROGRAM: Cyber

Background/Program Objectives: Under the Next Generation Cyber Initiative, Cyber Division (CyD) has realigned from a regional identification to a threat-based model, which enables it to focus on the greatest cyber threat to our national security - intrusions into government and private computer networks. To facilitate its mission of countering cyber threats, the FBI focuses its resources on targeting and disrupting the top cyber threat actors, leveraging its workforce, as well as developing and utilizing the latest technology to counter emerging trends.

In order to protect government and private computer networks from cyber intrusion, the CyD targets its resources on effectively disrupting and/or dismantling threat actors. Disruptions are milestones in the process of dismantling a group or organized criminal enterprise. Disruptions force an organization to adopt unfamiliar patterns or to use less experienced personnel creating opportunities for additional disruptions, and building momentum for the ultimate goal of the dismantlement of the organization. Dismantlements mean that the targeted organization's leadership, financial base and supply network has been destroyed, such that the organization is incapable of operating and/or reconstituting itself.

Performance Measure: Number of Computer Intrusion Program Disruptions and Dismantlements

> ***FY 2014 Actual Performance:*** 2,492
>
> ***FY 2015 Target:*** 500
>
> ***FY 2015 Actual Performance:*** 479

Discussion of FY 2015 Results:

The FBI manages cyber disruptions and dismantlement operations with the goal of eliminating the capabilities of a threat enterprise/organization engaged in criminal or national security related activities. During FY 2015, CyD successfully achieved more than 400 computer intrusion program disruptions and dismantlements against adversaries targeting global U. S. interests. Although CyD did not achieve the FY 2015 target of 500, the FBI made noteworthy progress towards neutralizing global cybercrime. For example, in July 2015 the FBI, in coordination with 19 foreign law enforcement partners, dismantled a computer hacking forum known as Darkode. Darkode was an online, password-protected forum where computer hackers and other cyber criminals assembled to buy, sell, trade and share information, ideas, and tools to facilitate unlawful intrusions on victims' computers and electronic devices.

Throughout FY 2015, CyD, in coordination with other law enforcement agencies and members of the IC, gathered evidence of computer intrusion techniques, patterns of criminal activity, and copies of malicious software. When possible, the FBI notified victims of computer intrusions, which enabled them to protect themselves against such tactics. In many circumstances victims were unaware their networks had been compromised. The FBI's information sharing and analysis capabilities have ensured that computer intrusion information and other information about cyber threats are also shared with other agencies in support of their independent cyber-related missions.

Although the total number of disruptions and dismantlements against criminal and national security related cyber threats is unpredictable because of the nature of ongoing cyber campaigns, the FBI expects continued and sustained performance on this metric.

STRATEGIC GOAL 2: Prevent Crime, Protect the Rights of the American People, and Enforce Federal Law *38 percent of the FBI's Net Cost supports this Goal.*

PROGRAM: Criminal Enterprises

Background/Program Objectives: The FBI's criminal enterprise investigations, managed by the Criminal Investigative Division at FBI Headquarters, focus on violent gangs, drug trafficking organizations (DTOs), and other organized violent criminal actors.

Gangs/Criminal Enterprises – Consolidated Priority Organization Target (CPOT) DTOs
In FY 2003, DOJ developed a single national list of criminal enterprises engaged in major drug trafficking and money laundering organizations. This list of targets, the CPOT list, is updated periodically and reflects the most significant international narcotic suppliers (and related money-laundering organizations), poly-drug traffickers, clandestine drug manufacturers and producers, and major drug transporters supplying the U.S.

The FBI has developed a comprehensive counter-drug strategy designed to investigate and prosecute illegal drug traffickers and distributors, reduce drug related crime and violence, provide assistance to other law enforcement agencies, and strengthen international cooperation. The strategy focuses the FBI's counter-drug resources on identified CPOT organizations associated primarily with Colombian, Mexican, and Caribbean drug trafficking organizations with the most adverse impact on U.S. national interests.

Performance Measure: CPOT-linked DTOs Dismantled

> ***FY 2014 Actual Performance:*** 31
>
> ***FY 2015 Target:*** 20
>
> ***FY 2015 Actual Performance:*** 34

Discussion of FY 2015 Results:

The FBI exceeded its FY 2015 goals and increased performance again this fiscal year for the number of CPOT linked organizations disrupted or dismantled compared to FY 2014. It is anticipated the FBI will continue to achieve greater efficiency linking cases to CPOTs that were not previously identified or documented; therefore, allowing higher documented production. The OCDETF continued to focus more resources toward CPOT linked investigations thereby increasing CPOT links and subsequent disruptions and dismantlements. Through continued education efforts with the field, as well as the correlation of CPOT linking to the approval of case funding requests; the FBI continues to increase OCDETF cases thus CPOT case linkages. To fully engage the field in support of the FBI's initiative to increase CPOT linkages, the OCDETF routinely provided communications outreach and instruction to the field by utilizing the Regional OCDETF Coordinators (ROCs), OCDETF Program Analysts (PAs), as well as, the substantive units at Headquarters in the Transnational Organized Crime Western Hemisphere, Eastern Hemisphere, and the Safe Streets and Gang Units.

Performance Measure: CPOT-linked DTOs Disrupted

> ***FY 2014 Actual Performance:*** 150
>
> ***FY 2015 Target:*** 40
>
> ***FY 2015 Actual Performance:*** 136

Discussion of FY 2015 Results:

The FBI exceeded its FY 2015 goals again this fiscal year for the number of CPOT linked organizations disrupted or dismantled compared to FY 2014. It is anticipated the FBI will continue to achieve greater efficiency linking cases to CPOTs that were not previously identified or documented; therefore, allowing higher documented production.

<u>Violent Gang Criminal Enterprises (VGCEs)</u>

The mission of the FBI's Violent Gang Program is to address the VGCE threat in the U.S. by aggressively identifying, prioritizing, and targeting the most violent street and prison gangs whose activities constitute criminal enterprises. In January 1992, the FBI established the Safe Streets Violent Crime Initiative to attack gang and drug-related violence through the establishment of long-term, proactive, and coordinated teams of federal, state, and local law enforcement officers and prosecutors. The teams are manifested in Violent Gang Safe Streets Task Forces (VGSSTFs). As of September 30, 2015, the 164 VGSSTFs managed by the FBI were comprised of approximately 891 FBI Special Agents and 1,695 state, local, and other federal law enforcement officials.

Through VGSSTFs, the FBI pursues violent gangs through sustained, proactive, and coordinated investigations and prosecutes gang members for a number of violations that include, but are not limited to, racketeering, drug conspiracy, and firearms violations. The Safe Streets Task Forces (SSTFs) concept expands cooperation and communication among federal, state, and local law enforcement agencies, increasing productivity and avoiding duplication of investigative efforts. SSTFs combine short-term, street-level enforcement activity with sophisticated investigative techniques such as undercover operations and Title III wire taps to root out, prosecute, and disrupt and dismantle the entire gang, from the street-level enforcers and dealers to crew leaders and the gang's command structure.

State and local officers bring an unparalleled level of expertise and knowledge regarding local gangs, gang members, and violent offenders operating in their department's area of responsibility. This knowledge, combined with FBI resources, ensures VGSSTFs are successful in disrupting and dismantling the most violent gangs.

Performance Measure: Number of Gangs/Criminal Enterprise Dismantlements (non-CPOT)

FY 2014 Actual Performance: 167
FY 2015 Target: 150
FY 2015 Actual Performance: 153

Discussion of FY 2015 Results:

The FBI met and exceeded its target for this measure in FY 2015 through sustained, proactive, coordinated investigations utilizing sophisticated techniques and technological advances. Combining short term, street-level enforcement activity with investigative techniques such as consensual monitoring, financial analysis and Title III wire intercepts, the FBI made significant achievements against the gang and criminal enterprise threat in FY 2015.

PROGRAM: White-Collar Crime (WCC)

Background/Program Objectives: The FBI's WCC program investigates criminals and criminal enterprises that seek illicit gains through fraud and guile. Illegal activities investigated include corporate, health care, securities and commodities, financial institution, mortgage, government (defense procurement and other areas), insurance, mass marketing, and bankruptcy fraud; environmental crimes; and money laundering.

U.S. citizens and businesses lose billions of dollars each year to criminals engaged in non-violent fraudulent enterprises. The globalization of economic and financial systems, technological advances, declining corporate and individual ethics, and the sophistication of criminal organizations have resulted in annual increases in the number of illegal acts characterized by deceit, concealment, or violations of trust. These crimes contribute to a loss of confidence in financial institutions, public institutions, and industry.

Performance Measure: Number of Criminal Enterprises Engaging in White-Collar Crimes Dismantled

> *FY 2014 Actual Performance:* 464
>
> *FY 2015 Target:* 368
>
> *FY 2015 Actual Performance:* 416

Discussion of FY 2015 Results:

The FBI met and exceeded its target for this measure in FY 2015 through proactive investigative techniques and technological advances. Increased utilization of advanced techniques not commonly utilized in past WCC cases enabled significant investigative achievements against WCC threat actors.

STRATEGIC GOAL 3: Ensure and Support the Fair, Impartial, Efficient, and Transparent Administration of Justice at the Federal, State, Local, Tribal, and International Levels *4 percent of the FBI's Net Cost supports this Goal.*

The FBI has no required reportable performance measures for Strategic Goal 3.

ANALYSIS OF SYSTEMS, CONTROLS, AND LEGAL COMPLIANCE

Federal Managers' Financial Integrity Act of 1982

The Federal Managers' Financial Integrity Act of 1982 (Integrity Act or FMFIA) provides the statutory basis for management's responsibility for and assessment of internal accounting and administrative controls. Such controls include program, operational, and administrative areas, as well as accounting and financial management. The Integrity Act requires federal agencies to establish controls that reasonably ensure obligations and costs are in compliance with applicable law; funds, property, and other assets are safeguarded against waste, loss, unauthorized use, or misappropriation; and revenues and expenditures are properly recorded and accounted for to maintain accountability over the assets. The Integrity Act also requires agencies to annually assess and report on the internal controls that protect the integrity of federal programs (FMFIA Section 2) and whether financial management systems conform to related requirements (FMFIA Section 4).

Internal Controls Program

Management of the FBI is responsible for establishing and maintaining effective internal controls and financial management systems that meet the objectives of the FMFIA. In accordance with OMB Circular A-123, *Management's Responsibility for Internal Control*, the FBI conducted its annual assessment of the effectiveness of internal controls to support effective and efficient programmatic operations, reliable financial reporting, and compliance with applicable laws and regulations (FMFIA Section 2). The FBI also assessed whether its financial management systems conform to financial systems requirements (FMFIA Section 4). Based on the results of the assessments, the FBI provided reasonable assurance that its internal controls and financial management systems met the objectives of the FMFIA, with the exception of the reportable condition summarized below. A Corrective Action Plan was established to institute programs and/or controls to eliminate this condition.

FMFIA Section 2 – Reportable Conditions

The FBI designated National Security Letters (NSLs) under Section 2 as a reportable condition. In March 2007, the Office of the Inspector General (OIG) reported that the FBI's use of NSLs grew dramatically and shifted in focus since the enactment of the Patriot Act and that NSLs served as an indispensable investigative tool. The OIG found issues with the FBI's tracking, reporting, and guidance regarding NSL usage. A March 2008 follow-up review assessed the FBI's corrective actions and indicated the FBI and the Department had made significant progress in implementing the 2007 recommendations. Improvements included strengthening the controls and automated workflow governing the request, review, and approval of NSLs; field office monthly reconciliations of NSL usage; and improving the database used to track NSL use. The FBI's actions to remediate the March 2007 OIG findings were completed by June 2007. The FBI agreed to each of the recommendations proposed in the 2008 report and implemented the proposed changes where appropriate. Several of the recommendations, however, were rendered moot by the FBI's implementation of the NSL Subsystem. An August 2014 report on the FBI's progress in the implementation of recommendations from 2007 and 2009 reviews resulted in 11 additional recommendations. The FBI continues to dedicate personnel and resources to ensure appropriate use of NSLs and to provide responses to OIG recommendations as necessary.

OMB Circular A-123, Appendix A – Internal Control Over Financial Reporting

In FY 2015, the FBI documented and assessed its significant business processes according to the requirements of DOJ's Implementation Plan for compliance with OMB Circular A-123, *Management's Responsibility for Internal Control*, revised December 21, 2004. The revised Circular A-123 re-examined internal control requirements for federal agencies in light of the requirements for publicly-traded companies implemented by the Sarbanes-Oxley Act of 2002. The full Circular A-123, *Appendix A: Internal Control Over Financial Reporting* assessment covered all processes deemed to be significant to the FBI and the DOJ. These processes were: Budget and Funds Management; Revenue and Receivables Management; Procurement; Property Management; Treasury and Fund Balance with Treasury; Human Resources; Financial Reporting; and Information Systems. The results of the assessment indicated no material weaknesses in the FBI's internal control over financial reporting as of June 30, 2015.

Federal Financial Management Improvement Act of 1996

The Federal Financial Management Improvement Act of 1996 (FFMIA or Act) was designed to improve federal financial and program managers' accountability, provide better information for decision-making, and improve the efficiency and effectiveness of federal programs. FFMIA requires agencies to have financial management systems that substantially comply with federal financial management systems requirements, applicable federal accounting standards, and the application of the U.S. Standard General Ledger (USSGL) at the transaction level. Furthermore, the Act requires independent auditors to report on agency compliance with the three requirements in the financial statement audit report. The Federal Information Security Management Act states that to be substantially compliant with FFMIA, there are to be no significant deficiencies in information security policies, procedures, or practices.

FFMIA Compliance Determination

The deployment of DOJ's UFMS system in October 2013 enabled the FBI to fully comply with all FFMIA requirements by utilizing the USSGL at the transaction level and integrating business data and activities through the elimination of subsystems such as the Available Funds File, the Procurement Module of FMS, and the Reimbursable Agreement Management System. UFMS is designed to meet the FBI's specific business requirements, while at the same time meet DOJ's goal of standardizing processes across the Department.

Legal Compliance

Except as discussed above, the FBI is not aware of any additional instances of material noncompliance with laws or regulations identified in OMB guidance, or with any laws or regulations that have a direct and material effect on the FBI's financial statements.

IMPROPER PAYMENTS INFORMATION ACT OF 2002, AS AMENDED

In accordance with OMB Circular A-123, Appendix C, *Requirements for Effective Estimation and Remediation of Improper Payments*, and the Departmental guidance for implementing the Improper Payments Information Act of 2002 (IPIA), as amended, the Department implemented a top-down approach to assess the risk of significant improper payments across all five of the Department's mission-aligned programs, and to identify and recapture improper payments through a payment recapture audit program. The approach promotes consistency across the Department and enhances internal control related to preventing, detecting, and recovering improper payments. Because of the OMB requirement to assess risk and report payment recapture audit activities by agency programs, the results of the Department's risk assessment and recapture activities are reported at the Department-level only.

In accordance with the Departmental approach for implementing IPIA, as amended, the FBI assessed its activities for susceptibility to significant improper payments and conducted its payment recapture audit program. The FBI provided the results of both the risk assessment and payment recapture audit activities to the Department for the Department-level reporting in the FY 2015 Agency Financial Report.

POSSIBLE FUTURE EFFECTS OF EXISTING EVENTS AND CONDITIONS

Factors and Future Trends Affecting Federal Bureau of Investigation Programs' Goal Achievement

The Changing Threat

Threats from the Islamic State, the increase in violent crime in the U.S., and the Office of Personnel Management (OPM) breach are all manifestations of the various threats the FBI faces and will continue to face in the near future. The FBI continues to identify individuals who seek to join the ranks of foreign fighters traveling in support of the Islamic State of Iraq and the Levant, commonly known as ISIL, and also homegrown violent extremists who may aspire to attack the U.S. from within. These threats remain among the highest priorities for the FBI and the IC as a whole.

The cyber threats to the U.S.'s national and economic security are becoming more diverse, sophisticated and harmful. Significant advances in global technological markets over the past few years have increased the risk of the FBI's technical capabilities falling significantly behind those of our adversaries. To avert this risk and to enhance the FBI's capabilities to combat rapidly changing cyber threats, the FBI has focused the efforts of the CyD on the greatest cyber threat – intrusions into government and industry computers and networks.

The WMD Directorate (WMDD) has seen an uptick in individuals interested in producing or using biological toxins in the U.S., likely influenced by popular media references glorifying the use of biological toxins in single-target murder plots. Since December 2013, criminal lone actors have increasingly exploited black market websites to sell and acquire biological toxins and chemicals for use in attacks targeting specific individuals.

Criminal threats continue in areas such as gang violence, transnational organized crime, civil rights, crimes against children, Indian country, fugitives, transportation crimes, and Southwest border.

Travel Request Initiation and Payment (TRIP)

The FBI's enterprise-wide TRIP system completed its second full year of use in FY 2015, processing over 150,000 Bureau travel requests. It has proven to be a stable, high-performing system that has improved the consistency and accuracy of travel submissions and payments, while increasing transparency to the travel reimbursement process. TRIP capabilities allowed the FBI to begin the consolidation of travel payment operations in Pocatello, ID in FY 2015. When completed, the consolidation of travel operations from individual field offices and divisions to Pocatello will reduce the FBI's voucher payment footprint from 300 to 30 employees. In addition, consolidation will ensure more uniform application of travel policy pertaining to travel reimbursements and provide greater opportunity for audit of travel payments. The FBI will continue to incrementally improve TRIP by implementing new functionality requested by users, correcting any errors as they are identified, and adding capabilities, such as increased reporting.

Budget Environment

While the threats facing the U.S. continue to evolve, the FBI and the rest of the federal government must operate within resource constraints. In accordance with administration guidance, the FBI has taken many steps to effectively operate within its resource constraints. The FBI continues to identify opportunities to modernize operations and to automate and streamline processes. Such innovations include:

- Implementation of new space allocation standards, consolidate special purpose rooms, and reduce the anticipated growth factor for facilities. The FBI also reduced the standard furniture workstation size and is currently in the process of researching and acquiring standard benching workstations to further increase space density.
- Contractor conversions into less expensive government positions.

Hiring

The FBI is aggressively pursuing and processing qualified candidates to fill vacant positions. The FBI has participated in hundreds of career fairs during FY 2015, targeting minority candidates, those with specialized skills (e.g. language, legal, financial), and other top quality individuals. These aggressive recruiting efforts are intended to address the large number of vacancies that accumulated due to the hiring freeze during the FY 2014 sequester, external hiring mandates, targeted retirement buyouts, and the contractor conversion process. However, progress in getting new employees on board has been slowed due to the large pool of candidates that entered the hiring process during a short time period time, creating a backlog, and the stringent selection process, which includes a requirement for candidates to pass a drug test, polygraph examination, and background investigation. The FBI will continue to utilize all available internal resources to surge support to short-staffed program activities, and to prioritize hiring for critical position vacancies, such as Special Agents and Intelligence Analysts, to mitigate this situation.

LIMITATIONS OF THE FINANCIAL STATEMENTS

The financial statements have been prepared to report the financial position and results of operations of the FBI, pursuant to the requirements of 31 U.S.C. 3515(b).

While the statements have been prepared from the books and records of the FBI in accordance with U.S. generally accepted accounting principles for federal entities and the formats prescribed by OMB, the statements are in addition to the financial reports used to monitor and control budgetary resources which are prepared from the same books and records.

The statements should be read with the realization that they are for a component of the U.S. government, a sovereign entity.

This page intentionally left blank.

U.S. DEPARTMENT OF JUSTICE

FEDERAL BUREAU OF INVESTIGATION

INDEPENDENT AUDITOR'S REPORTS

This page intentionally left blank.

INDEPENDENT AUDITOR'S REPORT ON THE FINANCIAL STATEMENTS

Inspector General
U.S. Department of Justice

Director
Federal Bureau of Investigation
U.S. Department of Justice

Report on the Financial Statements

We have audited the accompanying consolidated financial statements of the U.S. Department of Justice Federal Bureau of Investigation (FBI), which comprise the consolidated balance sheet as of September 30, 2015, the related consolidated statements of net cost and changes in net position, and the combined statement of budgetary resources for the year then ended; as well as the related notes to the consolidated financial statements.

Management's Responsibility for the Financial Statements

Management is responsible for the preparation and fair presentation of these consolidated financial statements in accordance with accounting principles generally accepted in the United States of America; this includes the design, implementation, and maintenance of internal control relevant to the preparation and fair presentation of consolidated financial statements that are free from material misstatement, whether due to fraud or error.

Auditor's Responsibility

Our responsibility is to express an opinion on these consolidated financial statements based on our audit. We conducted our audit in accordance with auditing standards generally accepted in the United States of America; the standards applicable to financial audits contained in *Government Auditing Standards*, issued by the Comptroller General of the United States; and Office of Management and Budget (OMB) Bulletin No. 15-02, *Audit Requirements for Federal Financial Statements*. Those standards and OMB Bulletin No. 15-02 require that we plan and perform the audit to obtain reasonable assurance about whether the consolidated financial statements are free from material misstatement.

An audit involves performing procedures to obtain audit evidence about the amounts and disclosures in the consolidated financial statements. The procedures selected depend on the auditor's judgment, including the assessment of the risks of material misstatement of the consolidated financial statements, whether due to fraud or error. In making those risk assessments, the auditor considers internal control relevant to the entity's preparation and fair presentation of the consolidated financial statements in order to design audit procedures that are appropriate in the circumstances, but not for the purpose of expressing an opinion on the effectiveness of the entity's internal control. Accordingly, we express no such opinion. An audit also includes evaluating the appropriateness of accounting policies used and the reasonableness of significant accounting estimates made by management, as well as evaluating the overall presentation of the consolidated financial statements.

We believe that the audit evidence we have obtained is sufficient and appropriate to provide a basis for our audit opinion.

Opinion

In our opinion, the consolidated financial statements referred to above present fairly, in all material respects, the financial position of the FBI as of September 30, 2015, and its net cost of operations, changes in net position, and budgetary resources for the year then ended, in accordance with accounting principles generally accepted in the United States of America.

Other Matters

Fiscal Year 2014 Financial Statements Audited by a Predecessor Auditor

The FBI's consolidated financial statements for fiscal year (FY) 2014 as of and for the year ended September 30, 2014 were audited by a predecessor auditor whose report, dated November 4, 2014, expressed an unmodified opinion on those consolidated financial statements. We were not engaged to audit, review, or apply any procedures on those consolidated financial statements. Accordingly, we do not express an opinion or any other form of assurance on the FY 2014 financial statements as a whole.

Required Supplementary Information

Accounting principles generally accepted in the United States of America require that the Management's Discussion and Analysis, and Required Supplementary Information (hereinafter referred to as the "required supplementary information") be presented to supplement the consolidated financial statements. Such information, although not a part of the consolidated financial statements, is required by OMB and the Federal Accounting Standards Advisory Board, who consider it to be an essential part of financial reporting for placing the consolidated financial statements in an appropriate operational, economic, or historical context. We have applied certain limited procedures to the required supplementary information in accordance with auditing standards generally accepted in the United States of America, which consisted of inquiries of management about the methods of preparing the information and comparing the information for consistency with management's responses to our inquiries, the consolidated financial statements, and other knowledge we obtained during our audit of the consolidated financial statements. We do not express an opinion or provide any assurance on the information because the limited procedures do not provide us with sufficient evidence to express an opinion or provide any assurance.

Other Information

Our audit was conducted for the purpose of forming an opinion on the consolidated financial statements as a whole. The Combined Schedules of Spending is presented for purposes of additional analysis and is not a required part of the consolidated financial statements. Such information has not been subjected to the auditing procedures applied in the audit of the consolidated financial statements; accordingly, we do not express an opinion or provide any assurance on it.

Other Reporting Required by Government Auditing Standards

In accordance with *Government Auditing Standards* and OMB Bulletin No. 15-02, we have also issued reports, dated November 4, 2015, on our consideration of the FBI's internal control over financial reporting and on our tests of the FBI's compliance with certain provisions of laws, regulations, contracts, and other matters for the year ended September 30, 2015. The purpose of those reports is to describe the scope of our testing of internal control over financial reporting and compliance and the results of that testing, and not to provide an opinion on internal control over financial reporting or on compliance and other matters. Those reports are an integral part of an audit performed in accordance with *Government Auditing Standards* and OMB Bulletin No. 15-02 in considering the FBI's internal control over financial reporting and compliance.

Kearney & Company

Alexandria, Virginia
November 4, 2015

This page intentionally left blank.

INDEPENDENT AUDITOR'S REPORT ON INTERNAL CONTROL OVER FINANCIAL REPORTING BASED ON AN AUDIT OF FINANCIAL STATEMENTS PERFORMED IN ACCORDANCE WITH *GOVERNMENT AUDITING STANDARDS*

Inspector General
U.S. Department of Justice

Director
Federal Bureau of Investigation
U.S. Department of Justice

We have audited the consolidated financial statements of the U.S. Department of Justice Federal Bureau of Investigation (FBI), which comprise the consolidated balance sheet as of September 30, 2015, the related consolidated statements of net cost and changes in net position, and the combined statement of budgetary resource for the year then ended, as well as the related notes to the consolidated financial statements, and have issued our report thereon dated November 4, 2015. We conducted our audit in accordance with auditing standards generally accepted in the United States of America; the standards applicable to financial audits contained in *Government Auditing Standards*, issued by the Comptroller General of the United States; and Office of Management and Budget (OMB) Bulletin No. 15-02, *Audit Requirements for Federal Financial Statements*.

Internal Control over Financial Reporting

In planning and performing our audit of the consolidated financial statements as of and for the year ended September 30, 2015, we considered the FBI's internal control over financial reporting (internal control) to determine the audit procedures that are appropriate in the circumstances for the purpose of expressing our opinion on the consolidated financial statements, but not for the purpose of expressing an opinion on the effectiveness of the FBI's internal control. Accordingly, we do not express an opinion on the effectiveness of the FBI's internal control. We limited our internal control testing to those controls necessary to achieve the objectives described in OMB Bulletin No. 15-02. We did not test all internal controls relevant to operating objectives as broadly defined by the *Federal Managers' Financial Integrity Act of 1982*, such as those controls relevant to ensuring efficient operations.

A deficiency in internal control exists when the design or operation of a control does not allow management or employees, in the normal course of performing their assigned functions, to prevent, or detect and correct, misstatements on a timely basis. A material weakness is a deficiency, or a combination of deficiencies, in internal control, such that there is a reasonable possibility that a material misstatement of the entity's financial statements will not be prevented, or detected and corrected, on a timely basis. A significant deficiency is a deficiency, or a combination of deficiencies, in internal control that is less severe than a material weakness, yet important enough to merit attention by those charged with governance.

Our consideration of internal control was for the limited purpose described in the first paragraph of this section and was not designed to identify all deficiencies in internal control that might be material weaknesses or significant deficiencies. Given these limitations, during our audit, we did not identify any deficiencies in internal control that we consider to be material weaknesses. However, material weaknesses may exist that have not been identified.

We noted certain additional matters involving internal control over financial reporting that we will report to the FBI's management in a separate letter.

Purpose of this Report

The purpose of this report is solely to describe the scope of our testing of internal control and the results of that testing, and not to provide an opinion on the effectiveness of the FBI's internal control. This report is an integral part of an audit performed in accordance with *Government Auditing Standards* and OMB Bulletin No. 15-02 in considering the FBI's internal control. Accordingly, this communication is not suitable for any other purpose.

Kearney & Company

Alexandria, Virginia
November 4, 2015

INDEPENDENT AUDITOR'S REPORT ON COMPLIANCE AND OTHER MATTERS BASED ON AN AUDIT OF FINANCIAL STATEMENTS CONDUCTED IN ACCORDANCE WITH *GOVERNMENT AUDITING STANDARDS*

Inspector General
U.S. Department of Justice

Director
Federal Bureau of Investigation
U.S. Department of Justice

We have audited the consolidated financial statements of the U.S. Department of Justice Federal Bureau of Investigation (FBI), which comprise the consolidated balance sheet as of September 30, 2015, the related consolidated statements of net cost and changes in net position, and the combined statement of budgetary resource for the year then ended, as well as the related notes to the consolidated financial statements, and have issued our report thereon dated November 4, 2015. We conducted our audit in accordance with auditing standards generally accepted in the United States of America; the standards applicable to financial audits contained in *Government Auditing Standards*, issued by the Comptroller General of the United States; and Office of Management and Budget (OMB) Bulletin No. 15-02, *Audit Requirements for Federal Financial Statements*.

Compliance and Other Matters

As part of obtaining reasonable assurance about whether the FBI's consolidated financial statements are free from material misstatement, we performed tests of its compliance with certain provisions of laws, regulations, and contracts, noncompliance with which could have a direct and material effect on the determination of financial statement amounts; and provisions referred to in Section 803(a) of the *Federal Financial Management Improvement Act of 1996* (FFMIA). We limited our tests of compliance to these provisions and did not test compliance with all laws, regulations, and contracts applicable to the FBI. Providing an opinion on compliance with those provisions was not an objective of our audit, and accordingly, we do not express such an opinion. The results of our tests disclosed no instances of noncompliance or other matters that are required to be reported under *Government Auditing Standards* or OMB Bulletin No. 15-02.

The results of our tests of compliance with FFMIA disclosed no instances in which the FBI's financial management systems did not comply substantially with the Federal financial management system's requirements, applicable Federal accounting standards, or application of the United States Standard General Ledger at the transaction level.

Purpose of this Report

The purpose of this report is solely to describe the scope of our testing of compliance and the results of that testing, and not to provide an opinion on the FBI's compliance. This report is an integral part of an audit performed in accordance with *Government Auditing Standards* and OMB Bulletin No. 15-02 in considering the FBI's compliance. Accordingly, this communication is not suitable for any other purpose.

Kearney & Company

Alexandria, Virginia
November 4, 2015

U.S. DEPARTMENT OF JUSTICE

FEDERAL BUREAU OF INVESTIGATION

PRINCIPAL FINANCIAL STATEMENTS
AND RELATED NOTES

This page intentionally left blank.

U.S. Department of Justice
Federal Bureau of Investigation
Consolidated Balance Sheets
As of September 30, 2015 and 2014

Dollars in Thousands		2015		2014
ASSETS (Note 2)				
Intragovernmental				
Fund Balance with U.S. Treasury (Note 3)	$	4,271,474	$	3,479,026
Accounts Receivable (Note 5)		335,690		388,269
Other Assets (Note 9)		6,894		14,489
Total Intragovernmental		4,614,058		3,881,784
Cash and Monetary Assets (Note 4)		73,580		57,551
Accounts Receivable, Net (Note 5)		35,419		36,498
Inventory and Related Property, Net (Note 6)		-		9,748
General Property, Plant and Equipment, Net (Note 8)		2,763,048		2,852,468
Advances and Prepayments		77,319		11,887
Other Assets (Note 9)		1		42
Total Assets	$	**7,563,425**	$	**6,849,978**
LIABILITIES (Note 10)				
Intragovernmental				
Accounts Payable	$	125,860	$	172,566
Accrued Federal Employees' Compensation Act Liabilities		33,322		32,827
Custodial Liabilities (Note 19)		19		-
Other Liabilities (Note 14)		123,437		90,814
Total Intragovernmental		282,638		296,207
Accounts Payable		440,845		298,023
Actuarial Federal Employees' Compensation Act Liabilities		193,721		200,670
Accrued Payroll and Benefits		115,112		101,066
Accrued Annual and Compensatory Leave Liabilities		283,758		269,900
Environmental and Disposal Liabilities (Note 11)		12,137		11,407
Seized Cash and Monetary Instruments (Note 13)		33,179		33,616
Contingent Liabilities (Note 15)		2,864		11,147
Other Liabilities (Note 14)		18,865		7,761
Total Liabilities	$	**1,383,119**	$	**1,229,797**
NET POSITION				
Unexpended Appropriations	$	2,631,892	$	2,640,676
Cumulative Results of Operations		3,548,414		2,979,505
Total Net Position	$	**6,180,306**	$	**5,620,181**
Total Liabilities and Net Position	$	**7,563,425**	$	**6,849,978**

The accompanying notes are an integral part of these financial statements.

U.S. Department of Justice
Federal Bureau of Investigation
Consolidated Statements of Net Cost
For the Fiscal Years Ended September 30, 2015 and 2014

Dollars in Thousands

	FY	Gross Costs Intra-governmental	Gross Costs With the Public	Gross Costs Total	Less: Earned Revenues Intra-governmental	Less: Earned Revenues With the Public	Less: Earned Revenues Total	Net Cost of Operations (Note 16)
Goal 1	2015	$ 1,426,003	$ 3,884,339	$ 5,310,342	$ 263,571	$ 10,961	$ 274,532	$ 5,035,810
	2014	$ 1,610,242	$ 3,481,744	$ 5,091,986	$ 302,342	$ 7,803	$ 310,145	$ 4,781,841
Goal 2	2015	914,346	2,641,172	3,555,518	299,471	7,056	306,527	3,248,991
	2014	751,137	2,296,397	3,047,534	297,393	5,043	302,436	2,745,098
Goal 3	2015	290,555	669,779	960,334	410,888	171,794	582,682	377,652
	2014	284,534	634,305	918,839	330,135	165,566	495,701	423,138
Total	2015	$ 2,630,904	$ 7,195,290	$ 9,826,194	$ 973,930	$ 189,811	$ 1,163,741	$ 8,662,453
	2014	$ 2,645,913	$ 6,412,446	$ 9,058,359	$ 929,870	$ 178,412	$ 1,108,282	$ 7,950,077

Goal 1   Prevent Terrorism and Promote the Nation's Security Consistent with the Rule of Law
Goal 2   Prevent Crime, Protect the Rights of the American People, and Enforce Federal Law
Goal 3   Ensure and Support the Fair, Impartial, Efficient, and Transparent Administration of Justice at the Federal, State, Local, Tribal, and International Levels

Federal Bureau of Investigation

32

The accompanying notes are an integral part of these financial statements.

U.S. Department of Justice
Federal Bureau of Investigation
Consolidated Statements of Changes in Net Position
For the Fiscal Years Ended September 30, 2015 and 2014

Dollars in Thousands		2015		2014
Unexpended Appropriations				
Beginning Balances	$	**2,640,676**	$	**1,822,476**
Budgetary Financing Sources				
Appropriations Received		8,436,569		8,343,284
Appropriations Transferred-In/Out		(35,187)		(34,706)
Appropriations Used		(8,410,166)		(7,490,378)
Total Budgetary Financing Sources		**(8,784)**		**818,200**
Unexpended Appropriations	$	**2,631,892**	$	**2,640,676**
Cumulative Results of Operations				
Beginning Balances	$	**2,979,505**	$	**3,041,917**
Budgetary Financing Sources				
Appropriations Used		8,410,166		7,490,378
Nonexchange Revenues		21		29
Transfers-In/Out Without Reimbursement		548,515		(1,651)
Other Financing Sources				
Transfers-In/Out Without Reimbursement		25,800		112,458
Imputed Financing from Costs Absorbed				
by Others (Note 17)		257,696		294,644
Other Financing Sources		(10,836)		(8,193)
Total Financing Sources		**9,231,362**		**7,887,665**
Net Cost of Operations		**(8,662,453)**		**(7,950,077)**
Net Change		568,909		(62,412)
Cumulative Results of Operations	$	**3,548,414**	$	**2,979,505**
Net Position	$	**6,180,306**	$	**5,620,181**

The accompanying notes are an integral part of these financial statements.

Dollars in Thousands		2015		2014
Budgetary Resources:				
Unobligated Balance, Brought Forward, October 1	$	1,321,242	$	1,124,439
Recoveries of Prior Year Unpaid Obligations		225,535		197,730
Other Changes in Unobligated Balances		(39,791)		(38,515)
Unobligated Balance from Prior Year Budget Authority, Net		1,506,986		1,283,654
Appropriations (discretionary and mandatory)		8,989,686		8,345,443
Spending Authority from Offsetting Collections (discretionary and mandatory)		1,204,903		1,178,873
Total Budgetary Resources	S	**11,701,575**	S	**10,807,970**
Status of Budgetary Resources:				
Obligations Incurred (Note 18)	$	9,704,484	$	9,486,728
Unobligated Balance, End of Year:				
Apportioned		1,609,687		1,110,032
Unapportioned		387,404		211,210
Total Unobligated Balance, End of Year		1,997,091		1,321,242
Total Status of Budgetary Resources	S	**11,701,575**	S	**10,807,970**
Change in Obligated Balance:				
Unpaid Obligations:				
Unpaid Obligations, Brought Forward, October 1	$	2,783,840	$	2,425,794
Obligations Incurred		9,704,484		9,486,728
Outlays, Gross		(9,427,102)		(8,930,952)
Recoveries of Prior Year Unpaid Obligations		(225,535)		(197,730)
Unpaid Obligations, End of Year		2,835,687		2,783,840
Uncollected Payments:				
Uncollected Payments from Federal Sources, Brought Forward, October 1		(606,615)		(617,526)
Change in Uncollected Customer Payments from Federal Sources		69,389		10,911
Uncollected Customer Payments from Federal Sources, End of Year		(537,226)		(606,615)
Memorandum (non-add) Entries:				
Obligated Balance, Start of Year	S	**2,177,225**	S	**1,808,268**
Obligated Balance, End of Year	S	**2,298,461**	S	**2,177,225**
Budgetary Authority and Outlays, Net:				
Budgetary Authority, Gross (discretionary and mandatory)	$	10,194,589	$	9,524,316
Less: Actual Offsetting Collections (discretionary and mandatory)		1,274,292		1,189,784
Change in Uncollected Customer Payments from Federal Sources (discretionary and mandatory)		69,389		10,911
Budgetary Authority, Net (discretionary and mandatory)	S	**8,989,686**	S	**8,345,443**
Outlays, Gross (discretionary and mandatory)	$	9,427,102	$	8,930,952
Less: Actual Offsetting Collections (discretionary and mandatory)		1,274,292		1,189,784
Outlays, Net (discretionary and mandatory)		8,152,810		7,741,168
Less: Distributed Offsetting Receipts		(1,153)		3,360
Agency Outlays, Net (Discretionary and mandatory)	S	**8,153,963**	S	**7,737,808**

U.S. DEPARTMENT OF JUSTICE
FEDERAL BUREAU OF INVESTIGATION
NOTES TO THE FINANCIAL STATEMENTS
(DOLLARS IN THOUSANDS, EXCEPT AS NOTED)

1.   **Summary of Significant Accounting Policies**

A. Reporting Entity

The Federal Bureau of Investigation (FBI or Bureau), established in 1908, is an integral part of the Department of Justice (DOJ or the Department). The mission of the FBI is to protect and defend the United States (U.S.) against terrorist and foreign intelligence threats, to uphold and enforce the criminal laws of the U.S., and to provide leadership and criminal justice services to federal, state, local, and international agencies and partners. The Bureau also provides assistance to other federal, state, and local law enforcement agencies and the public at large. Assistance includes forensic services, training law enforcement officials, background investigations, name checks, fingerprint analyses, and cooperative criminal investigations.

The accompanying financial statements of the FBI include the following funds under the administrative and/or operational control of the FBI: appropriated single year, multi-year, and no-year Salaries and Expense (S&E) funds; and appropriated no-year Construction (CNST) funds. These funds include new appropriations, transfers of appropriations from other federal agencies, and the carry-over of prior years' unobligated balances for multi-year and no-year appropriated funds. The FBI also receives reimbursable funding from other agencies for services rendered.

B. Basis of Presentation

These financial statements have been prepared from the books and records of the FBI in accordance with U.S. generally accepted accounting principles issued by the Federal Accounting Standards Advisory Board and presentation guidelines in the Office of Management and Budget (OMB) Circular A-136, *Financial Reporting Requirements*. These financial statements are different from the financial reports prepared pursuant to OMB directives used to monitor and control the use of the FBI's budgetary resources. To ensure that the FBI financial statements are meaningful at the entity level and to enhance reporting consistency within the Department, Other Assets and Other Liabilities as defined by OMB Circular A-136 have been disaggregated on the balance sheet. These include from Other Assets, Advances and Prepayments with the Public; and from Other Liabilities, Accrued Federal Employees' Compensation Act Liabilities, Accrued Payroll and Benefits, Accrued Annual and Compensatory Leave Liabilities, Seized Cash and Monetary Instruments, and Contingent Liabilities.

C. Basis of Consolidation

The consolidated/combined financial statements include the accounts of the FBI. All significant proprietary intra-entity transactions and balances have been eliminated in consolidation. The Statements of Budgetary Resources are combined statements for Fiscal Years (FYs) 2015 and 2014, and as such, intra-entity transactions have not been eliminated. The consolidated financial statements do not include centrally administered assets and liabilities of the federal government

1. **Summary of Significant Accounting Policies (continued)**

as a whole, such as General Services Administration (GSA) owned property and equipment, and borrowings from the public by the U.S. Department of the Treasury (Treasury), which may in part be attributed to the FBI.

D. Basis of Accounting

Transactions are recorded on the accrual and budgetary bases of accounting. Under the accrual basis, revenues are recorded when earned and expenses are recorded when incurred, regardless of when cash is exchanged. Under the budgetary basis, however, funds availability is recorded based upon legal considerations and constraints. As a result, certain line items on the proprietary financial statements may not equal similar line items on the budgetary financial statements.

E. Non-Entity Assets

Non-entity assets represent assets temporarily controlled and administered by the FBI, but not available to the FBI as a financing source for operations. The FBI withholds state and local income taxes from taxable travel and transfer related expenses from FBI employees for subsequent disbursement to the applicable taxing authorities. Undisbursed withholdings at fiscal year-end are recorded as non-entity assets on the balance sheet with an offsetting liability. Cash temporarily held by the FBI as evidence for legal proceedings is also included on the balance sheet as a non-entity asset with an offsetting liability.

F. Fund Balance with U.S. Treasury and Cash

Fund balances with the Treasury primarily represent appropriated, revolving, and trust funds available to pay current liabilities and finance future authorized purchases of goods and services. Receipts are processed by commercial banks for deposit to individual accounts maintained at the Treasury. Treasury and other Treasury-designated disbursing officers process cash receipts and disbursements as directed by authorized FBI certifying officers. The FBI field offices and legal attachés maintain imprest and emergency funds to accommodate law enforcement cash requirements occurring outside normal banking system operating hours.

G. Accounts Receivable

Accounts receivable are established for reimbursable expenses incurred by the FBI in providing goods and services ordered by other entities. Intragovernmental accounts receivable represent amounts due from federal entities and agencies. Other receivables represent amounts due from state and local governments, individuals, and other non-federal entities.

The Allowance for Uncollectible Accounts calculation methodology is a percentage based on outstanding receivables weighted against the collection rate of those receivables. An analytical review is conducted annually to update the percentage applied to outstanding receivables. An invoice is deemed delinquent if it is unpaid after 30 days. Intragovernmental receivables are considered fully collectible.

1. Summary of Significant Accounting Policies (continued)

H. Inventory and Related Property

Prior to FY 2015, operating materials and supplies (OM&S) consisted of fuel, ammunition, spare aircraft parts, and office supplies as held for use and were valued at acquisition cost for financial statement purposes in accordance with the Federal Accounting Standard Advisory Board Statement of Federal Financial Accounting Standards (SFFAS) No. 3, *Accounting for Inventory and Related Property*. This guidance states that OM&S consists of tangible property to be consumed in normal operations and should be categorized, as either held for use, held in reserve for future use, or obsolete.

In FY 2015, the FBI modified its method for accounting for OM&S based on an analysis of SFFAS No. 3 and current FBI business processes. This analysis resulted in FBI making a management decision to switch from the consumption method and elect to record OM&S using the purchase method exception under SFFAS No. 3. Per SFFAS No. 3, an exception to the consumption method is provided when (1) the OM&S are not significant amounts (2) they are in the hands of the end users for use in normal operations, or (3) it is not cost-beneficial to apply the consumption method. The purchase method may be used if any of these circumstances exist. FBI elected to switch to the purchase method due to the fact that each of the three circumstances listed above are present.

I. General Property, Plant, and Equipment

DOJ Financial Management Policy Memorandum (FMPM) 13-12, *Capitalization of General Property, Plant and Equipment and Internal Use Software*, was implemented by the FBI in FY 2013. For financial statement purposes, the primary change related to the capitalization thresholds for real property including leasehold improvements, personal property, and internal use software (IUS) which resulted in a decrease to the overall Property, Plant, and Equipment (PP&E) balance in FY 2013.

Below are the capitalization thresholds:

Type of Property	Threshold
Real Property	$250
Personal Property	$50
Aircraft	$100
Internal Use Software	$5,000

With the exception of land, all general PP&E is capitalized when the cost of acquiring or improving the property meets the capitalization thresholds noted in the table above and has a useful life of two or more years. All general PP&E is depreciated or amortized, based on historical cost, using the straight-line method over the estimated useful life of the asset. The FBI calculates a salvage value of 10 percent or less for capitalized property. Land is capitalized regardless of its acquisition cost and is never depreciated.

Expenditures for property and equipment with an acquisition cost or individual asset recognition value less than the applicable threshold are charged to operating expenses as incurred. The FBI uses work-in-process (WIP) accounts to capitalize expenditures associated with on-going

1. Summary of Significant Accounting Policies (continued)

leasehold improvement projects, the on-going construction of facilities and equipment, and the development of IUS that meet FBI's capitalization thresholds. Upon completion of the project(s), the applicable costs are transferred from WIP to a depreciable asset.

While the FBI owns some land, buildings, and other structures, it leases its headquarters building, field office buildings, and warehouse space from the GSA. The FBI also leases office space from non-governmental entities, both in the U.S. and abroad.

J. Advances and Prepayments

Advances and prepayments classified as assets include funds disbursed to finance operations that exceed the total expenditures incurred. This amount also includes advances of funds to federal employees for official travel, and the balance of travel advances in excess of travel expenses claimed on reimbursement vouchers. When authorized by procurement regulations, payments made in advance of the FBI's receipt of goods and services are recorded as prepaid charges at the time of prepayment and recognized as expenditures/expense when the related goods and services are received. Advances and prepayments involving other federal agencies are classified as *Other Assets* on the balance sheet.

K. Seized Property

All property seized for forfeiture, including property with evidentiary value, is reported by the DOJ Assets Forfeiture Fund and Seized Asset Deposit Fund. The FBI has an established reporting threshold of $1 or more for Personal Property seized for evidentiary purposes. The FBI reports each seized personal property evidence record as a single unit of measure.

Cash in the custody of the FBI for evidentiary purposes is recognized as an asset on the balance sheet with an offsetting liability. Non-monetary valuable property held as evidence is disclosed in Note 7 at the appraised or fair market value at the time of the seizure and is not adjusted to any subsequent increases and decreases in estimated fair market value. It is not recognized as an asset on the balance sheet.

Quantities of illegal drugs and firearms held as evidence are disclosed in Note 7 in accordance with Statement of Federal Financial Accounting Standards (SFFAS) No. 3, *Accounting for Inventory and Related Property*, and Federal Financial Accounting and Auditing Technical Release No. 4, *Reporting on Non-Valued Seized and Forfeited Property*. Reported quantities of drugs include only substances over one kilogram (KG) that are laboratory-analyzed and confirmed.

L. Liabilities

Liabilities represent the amount of monies or other resources likely to be paid by the FBI as the result of a transaction or an event that has already occurred. However, absent proper budget authority, the FBI cannot pay a liability. Liabilities for which an appropriation has not been enacted are considered unfunded liabilities. As a result, there is no certainty that corresponding future appropriations will be enacted to liquidate these unfunded liabilities.

M. Contingencies and Commitments

The FBI is party to various administrative proceedings, legal actions, and claims. The balance sheet includes an estimated liability for those legal actions where management and the Chief

1. Summary of Significant Accounting Policies (continued)

Counsel consider adverse decisions "probable" and amounts are reasonably estimable. Legal actions where management and the Chief Counsel consider adverse decisions "probable" or "reasonably possible" and the amounts are reasonably estimable are disclosed in Note 15, Contingencies and Commitments. However, there are cases where amounts have not been accrued or disclosed because the amounts of the potential loss cannot be estimated or the likelihood of an unfavorable outcome is considered "remote."

N. Annual, Sick, and Other Leave

Annual leave and compensatory leave are expensed as earned with an offsetting liability. Liabilities are reduced as leave is taken. At the end of each fiscal quarter, the balance in the accrued annual leave liability account is adjusted to reflect valuation at current pay rates. To the extent current-year or prior-year appropriations are not available to fund annual and compensatory leave that is earned but not taken, funding will be obtained from future financing sources. Sick leave and other types of non-vested leave are expensed as taken.

O. Interest on Late Payments

Pursuant to the Prompt Payment Act of 1999 (31 U.S.C. 3901-3907), the FBI pays interest to commercial concerns for payments made after the payment due date. The payment due date is generally 30 days after the receipt of a valid invoice by the designated activity, or 30 days after the receipt and acceptance of the goods or services, whichever is later. Interest is computed on the principal amount due at the rate of interest established by the Secretary of the Treasury, and published in the Federal Register, for interest payments under section 12 of the Contract Disputes Act of 1978 (41 U.S.C. 611). Interest is paid for the period beginning one day after the principal payment due date and ending on the date on which the principal payment is made.

P. Retirement Plans

With few exceptions, employees of the Department are covered by one of the following retirement programs:

1) Employees hired before January 1, 1984, are covered by the Civil Service Retirement System (CSRS). The FBI contributes 7.0 percent of the gross pay for regular employees and 7.5 percent for law enforcement officers.

2) Employees hired January 1, 1984 or later, are covered by the Federal Employees Retirement System (FERS).

a) Employees hired January 1, 1984 through December 31, 2012, are covered by the FERS. The FBI contributes 13.2 percent of the gross pay for regular employees and for agents 28.8 percent for law enforcement officers.

b) Employees hired January 1, 2013 through December 31, 2013, are covered by the Federal Employees Retirement System-Revised Annuity Employees (FERS-RAE) System. The FBI contributes 11.1 percent of the gross pay for regular employees and 26.5 percent for law enforcement officers.

c) Employees hired January 1, 2014 or later are covered by the Federal Employees Retirement System-Further Revised Annuity Employees (FERS-FRAE). The FBI contributes

1.   **Summary of Significant Accounting Policies (continued)**

11.1 percent of the gross pay for regular employees and 26.5 percent for law enforcement officers.

The accompanying financial statements report expenses incurred by the FBI for required contributions made to retirement accounts administered by the Office of Personnel Management (OPM). All employees are eligible to contribute to the Federal Thrift Savings Plan (TSP). For employees covered by the FERS, FERS-RAE and FERS-FRAE, a TSP account is automatically established to which the FBI is required to contribute an additional 1.0 percent of gross pay and match employee contributions up to 4.0 percent. The FBI is not authorized to make automatic or matching contributions to the TSP for employees covered by the CSRS. The FBI's financial statements do not report CSRS or FERS assets, accumulated plan benefits, or unfunded liabilities, if any, which may be applicable to its employees. Such reporting is the responsibility of OPM. SFFAS No. 5, Accounting for Liabilities of the Federal Government, requires employing agencies to recognize the cost of pensions and other retirement benefits during their employees' active years of service. Refer to Note 17, Imputed Financing from Costs Absorbed by Others, for additional details.

The FBI recognizes an additional expense and an offsetting imputed financing source for FBI Pension and Other Retirement Benefits Expense not covered by employee and FBI contributions; this expense is ultimately paid by OPM. Refer to Note 17, Imputed Financing from Costs Absorbed by Others, for additional details.

Q. Federal Employee Compensation Benefits

The Federal Employees' Compensation Act (FECA) provides income and medical cost protection to covered federal civilian employees injured on the job, employees who have incurred a work-related occupational disease, and beneficiaries of any employee whose death is attributable to a job-related injury or occupational disease. Claims incurred for benefits for FBI employees under FECA are administered by the Department of Labor (DOL) and are ultimately paid by the FBI.

The total FECA liability has two components: (1) unpaid billings and (2) an amount of estimated unbilled claims. Unpaid billings represent claims already paid by the DOL, which have not yet been reimbursed by the FBI. There is generally a two-year delay in the processing of the DOL payments through DOJ to the FBI. The FBI reports the unpaid billings as Accrued FECA Liabilities.

Unbilled claims are estimated by the DOL by applying actuarial projections to incurred (both reported and unreported) claims. The DOL calculates the actuarial liability of the federal government for future compensation benefits, which includes the expected liability for death, disability, medical, and miscellaneous approved compensation costs. The liability is determined using the paid-losses extrapolation method calculated over the next 37-year period. This method uses historical benefit payment patterns related to a specific incurred period to predict the ultimate payments related to that period. The projected annual benefit payments were discounted to present value. The resulting federal government liability is then distributed by the DOL to the respective departments.

DOJ calculates and distributes each bureau's respective portion of the total DOJ actuarial liability that is recorded for reporting purposes only. The Actuarial FECA Liability constitutes an extended estimate of future costs that will be obligated against budgetary resources the fiscal year in which the cost is actually paid to DOL by DOJ and, subsequently, by the FBI.

1.   Summary of Significant Accounting Policies (continued)

R. Intragovernmental Activity

Intragovernmental costs and exchange revenues represent transactions made between two reporting entities within the federal government. Costs and exchange revenues with the public represent transactions made between the reporting entity and a non-federal entity. With the exception of certain accruals, the classification of revenue or cost as "intragovernmental" or "with the public" is defined on a transaction-by-transaction basis. The purpose of this classification is to enable the federal government to prepare consolidated financial statements, not to match public and intragovernmental revenue with the costs incurred to produce public and intragovernmental revenue.

S. Revenues and Other Financing Sources

The FBI receives funding to support its programs and executes its assigned mission from three primary sources: (1) annual, no-year, and multi-year appropriations by the U.S. Congress; (2) appropriated funds transferred to the FBI; and (3) reimbursable program funding. Appropriated funds (appropriated to the FBI or appropriated to other federal entities and transferred to the FBI for execution) represent the majority of the FBI's operating budget.

A source of revenue to the FBI are fees authorized by law for providing fingerprint-based and name-based Criminal History Record Information checks and other identification services submitted by authorized users for noncriminal justice purposes, including employment and licensing. The fee is based on full-cost recovery, determined by using an activity-based cost model. By law, the FBI may set such fees at a level to include an additional amount to establish a fund to defray expenses for the automation of fingerprint identification and criminal justice information services and associated costs. Fee schedules are announced in the Federal Register following a public comment period. The FBI is not authorized to charge fees for fingerprint identification and criminal justice information services for law enforcement purposes.

Other financing sources to the FBI include assets transferred to the FBI without reimbursement and imputed financing for: (1) FBI pension and other benefits expenses not covered by employee and FBI contributions and which are ultimately paid by OPM; and (2) expenses for legal claims paid out of the Treasury Judgment Fund on behalf of the FBI.

Appropriations are recognized as financing sources when the goods and services authorized to be paid from the appropriations have been received and accepted, or when program or administrative expenses have been incurred. Revenue from reimbursable activities is recognized when it is earned, i.e. when the goods or services ordered have been delivered or rendered to the ordering entity. The FBI also earns revenue from the sale of assets, principally vehicles.

T. Funds from Dedicated Collections

SFFAS No. 27, *Identifying and Reporting Funds from Dedicated Collections,* as amended defines 'funds from dedicated collections' as being financed by specifically identified revenues, provided to the government by non-federal sources, often supplemented by other financing sources, which remain available over time. These specifically identified revenues and other financing sources are required by statute to be used for designated activities, benefits, or purposes, and must be accounted for separately from the government's general revenues. The three required criteria for a fund from dedicated collections are:

1.   Summary of Significant Accounting Policies (continued)

1. A statute committing the federal government to use specifically identified revenues and/or other financing sources that are originally provided to the federal government by a non-federal source only for designated activities, benefits, or purposes;

2. Explicit authority for the funds to retain revenues and/or other financing sources not used in the current period for future use to finance the designated activities, benefits, or purposes; and

3. A requirement to account for and report on the receipt, use, and retention of the revenues and/or other financing sources that distinguishes the fund from the federal government's general revenues.

There are no funds that meet the definition of funds from dedicated collections.

U. Tax Exempt Status

As an agency of the federal government, the FBI is exempt from all income taxes imposed by any governing body whether it is a federal, state, commonwealth, local, or foreign government.

V. Use of Estimates

The preparation of financial statements requires management to make estimates and assumptions that affect the reported amounts of assets and liabilities and the reported amounts of revenue and expenses during the reporting period. Actual results could differ from those estimates.

W. Reclassifications

The FY 2014 financial statements were reclassified to conform to the FY 2015 Departmental and OMB financial statement presentation requirements. The reclassifications had no material effect on the total assets, liabilities, net position, changes in net position or budgetary resources previously reported.

X. Subsequent Events

Subsequent events and transactions occurring after September 30, 2015 through the date of the auditors' opinion have been evaluated for potential recognition or disclosure in the financial statements. The date of the auditors' opinion also represents the date that the financial statements were available to be issued.

2. Non-Entity Assets

Non-entity assets are assets that are held by the FBI but are not available for its use.

As of September 30, 2015 and 2014	2015	2014
Intragovernmental		
Fund Balance with U.S. Treasury	$ (1,156)	$ 21
With the Public		
Cash and Monetary Assets	50,658	38,230
Total Non-Entity Assets	49,502	38,251
Total Entity Assets	7,513,923	6,811,727
Total Assets	$ 7,563,425	$ 6,849,978

3. Fund Balance with U.S. Treasury

As of September 30, 2015 and 2014	2015	2014
Fund Balances		
General Funds	$ 4,272,630	$ 3,479,029
Other Fund Types	(1,156)	(3)
Total Fund Balances with U.S. Treasury	$ 4,271,474	$ 3,479,026
Status of Fund Balances		
Unobligated Balance - Available	$ 1,114,312	$ 1,110,032
Unobligated Balance - Available in Subsequent Periods	495,375	-
Unobligated Balance - Unavailable	387,404	211,210
Obligated Balance not yet Disbursed	2,298,461	2,177,225
Other Funds (With)/Without Budgetary Resources	(24,078)	(19,441)
Total Status of Fund Balances	$ 4,271,474	$ 3,479,026

The General Funds amount includes the remaining funds resulting from budget authority to pay valid obligations. Other Fund Types amount includes deposit, clearing, and suspense accounts temporarily held with Treasury until such time they are required for use.

Unobligated Balance - Available includes current year apportionments that may be used for new obligations. Unobligated Balance - Available in Subsequent Periods includes amounts apportioned for future fiscal years that are available for obligation in a subsequent period (apportioned as Category C). Unobligated Balance - Unavailable includes amounts appropriated in prior fiscal years that are no longer available to fund new obligations, but can be used for upward and/or downward adjustments for existing obligations. Obligated Balance not yet Disbursed includes obligations of appropriated funds and obligations related to reimbursable activity. Other Funds (With)/Without Budgetary Resources includes deposit, clearing, and suspense accounts.

4.   **Cash and Monetary Assets**

As of September 30, 2015 and 2014

	2015	2014
Cash		
Undeposited Collections	$ -	$ (118)
Imprest Funds	22,921	19,439
Other Cash	17,480	4,614
Total Cash	40,401	23,935
Monetary Assets		
Seized Monetary Instruments	33,179	33,616
Total Cash and Monetary Assets	$ 73,580	$ 57,551

Undeposited Collections includes various in-transit accounts where account activities have been processed in the FBI's Unified Financial Management System, but not deposited in the bank and reported to Treasury via the Classification Transactions and Accountability Report (formerly SF-224) monthly submission. The Undeposited Collections balance represents timing differences in the recording of transactions between the FBI and Treasury.

Imprest Funds reflects monies dedicated for operational support, such as petty cash and emergency funds.

Other Cash consists of project generated proceeds.

Seized Monetary Instruments represents cash evidence obtained during FBI investigations held pending release to the rightful owners.

5. Accounts Receivable, Net

As of September 30, 2015 and 2014

	2015	2014
Intragovernmental		
Accounts Receivable	$ 335,690	$ 388,269
With the Public		
Accounts Receivable	35,611	37,429
Allowance for Uncollectible Accounts	(192)	(931)
Total With the Public	35,419	36,498
Total Accounts Receivable, Net	$ 371,109	$ 424,767

Intragovernmental receivables are based on services provided to other federal agencies for activities such as name checks, requests for international travel, and training. The significant types of receivables reported in With the Public include the Non-Federal User Fee Program and the National Name Check Program. These customers are typically state and local government agencies conducting background checks on individuals.

6. Inventory and Related Property, Net

As of September 30, 2015 and 2014

	2015	2014
Operating Materials and Supplies		
Held for Current Use	$ -	$ 9,748

In FY 2015, the FBI modified its method for accounting for OM&S, from the consumption method to the purchase method, based on an analysis of SFFAS No. 3 and current FBI business processes (See note 1.H).

7. Seized Property, Net

Analysis of Change in Seized Property:

Seized Monetary Instruments (see also Notes 4 and 13) includes cash held by the FBI as evidence for legal proceedings, and is reported on the balance sheet as an asset, with an offsetting liability. Non-monetary evidence includes art, jewelry, and other valuables (see Note 1.K). According to DOJ guidelines, evidence items subject to forfeiture are not disclosed by the seizing agency.

The item counts and financial value of non-monetary valuable property in the custody of the FBI as of September 30, 2015 and 2014, excluding forfeited property for evidentiary purposes, and activity during

Federal Bureau of Investigation   45

These notes are an integral part of the financial statements.

7.   Seized Property, Net (continued)

each fiscal year are summarized in the following charts in accordance with SFFAS No. 3, *Accounting for Inventory and Related Property.*

Drug evidence is presented in accordance with Federal Financial Accounting and Auditing Technical Release No. 4, *Reporting on Non-Valued Seized and Forfeited Property.* Analyzed drug evidence represents actual laboratory-tested classification and weight in KG. Since enforcement of the controlled substances laws and regulations of the U.S. is incidental to the mission of the FBI, only individual seizures exceeding one KG in weight are reported.

"Other" primarily consists of substances, both controlled and non-controlled as defined per the Controlled Substances Act, other than cocaine, heroin, marijuana, or methamphetamine. The actual drug weight may vary from seizure weight due to changes in moisture content over time.

Unanalyzed drug evidence is not reported by the FBI because it is neither weighed nor confirmed by laboratory chemists. Seized drug evidence must be analyzed and confirmed through laboratory testing to be placed in one of the five categories of drugs above.

"Disposals" occur when evidence is either returned to the owner or destroyed in accordance with federal guidelines.

For the Fiscal Year Ended September 30, 2015

Seized Property Category		Beginning Balance	Adjustments**	Seizures	Disposals	Ending Balance
Seized for Evidence						
Seized Monetary Instruments	Value	$ 33,616	$ (6,334)	$ 10,683	$ (4,786)	$ 33,179
Personal Property	Number	350	(35)	75	(73)	317
	Value	$ 7,094	$ (2,595)	$ 2,325	$ (1,293)	$ 5,531
Non-Valued						
Firearms	Number	27,527	(157)	3,477	(2,588)	28,259
Drug Evidence						
Cocaine	KG	4,411	1,379	103	(240)	5,653
Heroin	KG	133	75	11	(1)	218
Marijuana	KG	1,020	73	251	(31)	1,313
Methamphetamine	KG	639	23	72	(37)	697
Other	KG	153	136	6	(5)	290
Total Drug Evidence		6,356	1,686	443	(314)	8,171

**Adjustments include property status and valuation changes received after, but properly credited to the prior fiscal year. Valuation changes include updates and corrections to an asset's value recorded in a prior year.

7. Seized Property, Net (continued)

For the Fiscal Year Ended September 30, 2014

Seized Property Category		Beginning Balance	Adjustments**	Seizures	Disposals	Ending Balance
Seized for Evidence						
Seized Monetary Instruments	Value	$ 46,371	$ (16,544)	$ 15,709	$ (11,920)	$ 33,616
Personal Property	Number	1,118	(728)	27	(67)	350
	Value	$ 27,422	$ (19,174)	$ 883	$ (2,037)	$ 7,094
Non-Valued						
Firearms	Number	28,917	(2,039)	3,284	(2,635)	27,527
Drug Evidence						
Cocaine	KG	6,362	(1,943)	152	(160)	4,411
Heroin	KG	414	(283)	15	(13)	133
Marijuana	KG	3,326	(2,116)	19	(209)	1,020
Methamphetamine	KG	873	(303)	106	(37)	639
Other	KG	1,032	(858)	-	(21)	153
Total Drug Evidence		12,007	(5,503)	292	(440)	6,356

**Adjustments include property status and valuation changes received after, but properly credited to the prior fiscal year. Valuation changes include updates and corrections to an asset's value recorded in a prior year.

Method of Disposition of Seized Property:

During FYs 2015 and 2014, $2,306 and $4,491, respectively, were returned to parties with a bonafide interest, and $3,773 and $9,466, respectively, were either released to a designated party or transferred to the appropriate federal entity under abandonment proceedings. Non-valued property was primarily disposed of through destruction.

8.   General Property, Plant and Equipment, Net

As of September 30, 2015

	Acquisition Cost	Accumulated Depreciation	Net Book Value	Useful Life
Land and Land Rights	$ 6,667	$ -	$ 6,667	N/A
Construction in Progress	350,658	-	350,658	N/A
Buildings, Improvements, and Renovations	798,390	(339,771)	458,619	10-50 years
Other Structures and Facilities	41,401	(19,875)	21,526	10-50 years
Aircraft	344,595	(98,922)	245,673	5-30 years
Boats	10,077	(3,625)	6,452	5-25 years
Vehicles	139,325	(96,740)	42,585	2-25 years
Equipment	761,145	(493,593)	267,552	2-25 years
Leasehold Improvements	678,185	(327,068)	351,117	3-10 years
Internal Use Software	1,615,830	(695,335)	920,495	3-7 years
Internal Use Software in Development	91,704	-	91,704	N/A
Total	$ 4,837,977	$ (2,074,929)	$ 2,763,048	

During FY 2015, the FBI purchased $94,044 in capital property from federal sources and $305,072 from the public.

As of September 30, 2014

	Acquisition Cost	Accumulated Depreciation	Net Book Value	Useful Life
Land and Land Rights	$ 8,167	$ -	$ 8,167	N/A
Construction in Progress	389,733	-	389,733	N/A
Buildings, Improvements, and Renovations	662,635	(316,747)	345,888	10-50 years
Other Structures and Facilities	41,401	(18,850)	22,551	10-50 years
Aircraft	302,584	(84,894)	217,690	5-30 years
Boats	10,287	(3,312)	6,975	5-25 years
Vehicles	128,111	(92,557)	35,554	2-25 years
Equipment	742,092	(439,303)	302,789	2-25 years
Leasehold Improvements	633,338	(268,005)	365,333	3-10 years
Internal Use Software	1,508,209	(431,558)	1,076,651	3-10 years
Internal Use Software in Development	81,137	-	81,137	N/A
Total	$ 4,507,694	$ (1,655,226)	$ 2,852,468	

During FY 2014, the FBI purchased $84,702 in capital property from federal sources and $351,273 from the public.

9.   Other Assets

As of September 30, 2015 and 2014	2015	2014
Intragovernmental		
Advances and Prepayments	$ 6,894	$ 14,489
Other Assets With the Public	1	42
Total Other Assets	$ 6,895	$ 14,531

Other Assets With the Public consist of cancelled US Treasury disbursements awaiting reissuance or cancellation by the FBI.

10.   Liabilities not Covered by Budgetary Resources

As of September 30, 2015 and 2014	2015	2014
Intragovernmental		
Accrued FECA Liabilities	$ 33,322	$ 32,827
Other Unfunded Employment Related Liabilities	130	193
Total Intragovernmental	33,452	33,020
With the Public		
Actuarial FECA Liabilities	193,721	200,670
Accrued Annual and Compensatory Leave Liabilities	283,758	269,900
Environmental and Disposal Liabilities (Note 11)	12,137	11,407
Contingent Liabilities (Note 15)	2,864	11,147
Total With the Public	492,480	493,124
Total Liabilities not Covered by Budgetary Resources	525,932	526,144
Total Liabilities Covered by Budgetary Resources	857,187	703,653
Total Liabilities	$ 1,383,119	$ 1,229,797

Liabilities not Covered by Budgetary Resources reports the receipt of goods and services, or eligible events in the current or prior periods, for which funds to pay the liabilities have not been made available through appropriations to the FBI.

11.   Environmental and Disposal Liabilities

In accordance with the Federal Accounting Standard Advisory Board's (FASAB) Statements of Federal Financial Accounting Standards (SFFAS) No. 5, *Accounting for Liabilities of the Federal Government*, SFFAS No. 6, *Accounting for Property, Plant, and Equipment*, Federal Financial Accounting and Auditing Technical Release No. 2, *Environmental Liabilities Guidance*, and Federal Financial Accounting and Auditing Technical Release No. 10, *Implementation Guidance on Asbestos Cleanup Costs Associated with Facilities and Installed Equipment* federal agencies are required to recognize liabilities for environmental cleanup costs when the future outflow or sacrifice of resources is probable and reasonably estimable.

As environmental-related cleanup costs are paid, the liabilities are reduced. Additionally, estimates will be revised periodically to account for material changes due to inflation, technology, and applicable laws and regulations. Any material changes in the estimated total cleanup costs will be expensed when estimates are revised and the liability balance adjusted.

As of September 30, 2015 and 2014	2015	2014
Firing Ranges		
Beginning Balance, Brought Forward	$ 831	$ -
Future Funded Expenses	495	831
Firing Range Liability	1,326	831
Asbestos		
Beginning Balance, Brought Forward	$ 10,576	$ 10,451
Abatements	-	(110)
Inflation Adjustment	2	2
Future Funded Expenses	233	233
Asbestos Liability	$ 10,811	$ 10,576
Total Environmental and Disposal Liabilities	$ 12,137	$ 11,407

Section 112 of the Clean Air Act requires the U.S. Environmental Protection Agency (EPA) to develop and enforce regulations to protect the general public from exposure to airborne contaminants known to be hazardous to human health. On March 31, 1971, the EPA identified asbestos as a hazardous pollutant, and on April 6, 1973, the EPA first promulgated the Asbestos National Emissions Standards for Hazardous Air Pollutants.

The FBI exercises due care in determining the presence of contamination in adherence to the law, rules and regulations, and policies of the Clean Air Act. The Facilities and Logistics Service Division, responsible for managing and maintaining FBI and non-FBI owned facilities, has identified FBI-owned facilities in Quantico that contain hazardous friable and non-friable asbestos. The facilities have a useful life of 50 years. The estimated total asbestos liability of $11,614 is based on the square footage of the facilities that may be contaminated. This value divided by the useful life and multiplied by the number of years in service, less any current year abatements, and adjusted for inflation is the estimated cleanup

11.   Environmental and Disposal Liabilities (continued)

liability. The estimated asbestos cleanup liability is increased each quarter by recording future funded expenses for the asbestos cleanup costs.

EPA's Statement on National Guidance EPA-902-B-01-001 discusses the potential environmental impacts of firing ranges. The Facilities and Logistics Service Division, responsible for managing and maintaining FBI and non-FBI owned facilities, has identified FBI-owned range facilities in Quantico and El Toro that contain possible contamination issues based on the Federal Financial Accounting and Auditing Technical Release No. 2, *Environmental Liabilities Guidance* and EPA-902-B-01-001. Due care requires the agency to exert a reasonable effort to identify the presence or likely presence of contamination. Since no remedial investigation/feasibility study (RI/FS) has been completed and there are no comparable sites, remediation costs are not considered reasonably estimable at this time. Technical Release No. 2, *Environmental Liabilities Guidance* then requires the agency to recognize the anticipated cost of conducting a future study, plus any other identifiable costs, as a future environmental and disposal liability.

The estimated total firing range liability of $1,326 is based on the estimated costs for contamination remediation. As of September 30, 2015 and 2014, the FBI reported the estimated firing range cleanup liability of $1,326 and $831, respectively.

There are no other potentially responsible parties to the environmental liability and there are no unrecognized amounts to disclose as of September 30, 2015.

12. Leases

The majority of space occupied by the FBI is leased from the GSA. The rental cost is based on the area occupied at the commercial rate per square foot, negotiated by the GSA along with appropriate GSA fees. The majority of the leases are cancelable; however, if tenant improvement (TI) costs are amortized in the lease and the FBI terminates prior to the end of the amortized period, the FBI will be responsible for the unpaid TI costs.

Typically, the minimum lease term for a Resident Agency (RA) is five years and the maximum is 15 years. The minimum lease term for a field office is 15 years and the maximum is 20 years. Some new leases for field offices and RAs will be noncancelable.

For field offices, lease terms that are scheduled to expire within the next five years are currently being analyzed. The FBI is in the process of relocating four field offices between 2016 and 2020 with the potential to relocate an additional five field offices if the requirements cannot be met at the existing locations. When field offices relocate, often from space leased for 20 years or longer, the rental rates increase significantly to accommodate the FBI's growth in workforce, space needs, and specialized security requirements.

As of September 30, 2015

Future Noncancelable Operating Lease Payments Due

Fiscal Year	Land and Buildings	Machinery and Equipment	Total
2016	201,736	-	201,736
2017	225,447	-	225,447
2018	231,202	-	231,202
2019	228,446	-	228,446
2020	219,295	-	219,295
After 2020	1,869,845	-	1,869,845
Total Future Noncancelable Operating Lease Payments	$ 2,975,971	$ -	$ 2,975,971

13. Seized Cash and Monetary Instruments

Seized Cash and Monetary Instruments represents liabilities for seized assets held by the FBI pending disposition. The Seized Cash and Monetary Instruments as of September 30, 2015 and 2014 are $33,179 and $33,616, respectively.

14. Other Liabilities

All Other Liabilities are current and presented in the following table:

As of September 30, 2015 and 2014

	2015	2014
Intragovernmental		
Employer Contributions and Payroll Taxes Payable	$ 38,804	$ 31,375
Other Post-Employment Benefits Due and Payable	78	113
Other Unfunded Employment Related Liabilities	130	193
Advances from Others	84,158	59,514
Liability for Clearing Accounts	(1,337)	(764)
Liability for Non-Entity Assets Not Reported on the Statement of Custodial Activity	1,604	383
Total Intragovernmental	123,437	90,814
With the Public		
Advances from Others	1,228	1,239
Liability for Nonfiduciary Deposit Funds and Undeposited Collections	(25)	(25)
Liability for Clearing Accounts	182	761
Other Liabilities	17,480	5,786
Total With the Public	18,865	7,761
Total Other Liabilities	$ 142,302	$ 98,575

15. Contingencies and Commitments

	Accrued Liabilities	Estimated Range of Loss Lower	Estimated Range of Loss Upper
As of September 30, 2015			
Probable	$ 2,864	$ 2,864	$ 6,294
Reasonably Possible	-	16,469	19,599
As of September 30, 2014			
Probable	$ 11,147	$ 11,147	$ 19,007
Reasonably Possible	-	13,119	16,944

16. Net Cost of Operations by Suborganization

The methodology by which the FBI allocates gross costs and earned revenue across the three Strategic Goals (SGs or Goal) is consistent with the methodology used to allocate the FBI's budget to the three SGs in the FY 2016 Authorization and Budget Request to Congress. The tables below and on the next page break out costs and revenue by these three SGs, as well as by FBI appropriation. These funds include new appropriations, transfers of appropriations from other federal agencies, and the carry-over of prior years' unobligated balances for multi-year and no-year appropriated funds.

For the Year Ended September 30, 2015

	Suborganizations		
	CNST	S&E	Consolidated
Goal 1: Prevent Terrorism and Promote the Nation's Security Consistent with the Rule of Law			
Gross Cost	$ 32,870	$ 5,277,472	$ 5,310,342
Less: Earned Revenue	-	274,532	$ 274,532
Net Cost of Operations	32,870	5,002,940	5,035,810
Goal 2: Prevent Crime, Protect the Rights of the American People, and Enforce Federal Law			
Gross Cost	$ 22,712	$ 3,532,806	$ 3,555,518
Less: Earned Revenue	-	306,527	$ 306,527
Net Cost of Operations	22,712	3,226,279	3,248,991
Goal 3: Ensure and Support the Fair, Impartial, Efficient, and Transparent Administration of Justice at the Federal, State, Local, Tribal, and International Levels			
Gross Cost	$ 5,375	$ 954,959	$ 960,334
Less: Earned Revenue	-	582,682	$ 582,682
Net Cost of Operations	5,375	372,277	377,652
Net Cost of Operations	$ 60,957	$ 8,601,496	$ 8,662,453

16. Net Cost of Operations by Suborganization (continued)

For the Fiscal Year Ended September 30, 2014

	Suborganizations		
	CNST	S&E	Consolidated
Goal 1: Prevent Terrorism and Promote the Nation's Security Consistent with the Rule of Law			
Gross Cost	$ 45,256	$ 5,046,730	$ 5,091,986
Less: Earned Revenue	-	310,145	310,145
Net Cost of Operations	45,256	4,736,585	4,781,841
Goal 2: Prevent Crime, Protect the Rights of the American People, and Enforce Federal Law			
Gross Cost	25,419	3,022,115	3,047,534
Less: Earned Revenue	-	302,436	302,436
Net Cost of Operations	25,419	2,719,679	2,745,098
Goal 3: Ensure and Support the Fair, Impartial, Efficient, and Transparent Administration of Justice at the Federal, State, Local, Tribal, and International Levels			
Gross Cost	8,119	910,720	918,839
Less: Earned Revenue	-	495,701	495,701
Net Cost of Operations	8,119	415,019	423,138
Net Cost of Operations	$ 78,794	$ 7,871,283	$ 7,950,077

17. Imputed Financing from Costs Absorbed by Others

Imputed Inter-Departmental Financing Sources are the unreimbursed (i.e. non-reimbursed and under-reimbursed) portion of the full costs of goods and services received by the FBI from a providing federal entity that is not part of the DOJ. In accordance with SFFAS No. 30, *Inter-Entity Cost Implementation Amending SFFAS 4, Managerial Cost Accounting Standards and Concepts,* the material Imputed Inter-Departmental Financing Sources recognized by the FBI are the cost of future benefits for the Federal Employees Health Benefits Program (FEHB), the Federal Employees Group Life Insurance Program (FEGLI), and the federal pension plans that are paid by other federal entities, and any unreimbursed payments made from the Treasury Judgment Fund on behalf of the FBI. The Treasury Judgment Fund was established by Congress and funded at 31 U.S.C. 1304 to pay in whole or in part the court judgments and settlement agreements negotiated by the Department on behalf of agencies, as well as certain types of administrative awards. Interpretation of Federal Financial Accounting Standards No. 2, *Accounting for Treasury Judgment Fund Transactions* requires agencies to recognize liabilities and expense when unfavorable litigation outcomes are probable and the amount can be estimated and will be paid by the Treasury Judgment Fund.

SFFAS No. 5 requires that employing agencies recognize the cost of pensions and other retirement benefits during their employees' active years of service. SFFAS No. 5 requires OPM to provide cost factors necessary to calculate cost. OPM actuaries calculate the value of pension benefits expected to be paid in the future, and then determine the total funds to be contributed by and for covered employees, such that the amount calculated would be sufficient to fund the projected pension benefits. The cost factors are as follows:

17.   Imputed Financing from Costs Absorbed by Others (continued)

	Category	Cost Factor (%)
Civil Services Retirement System (CSRS)	Regular Employees	33.4
	Regular Employees Offset	24.5
	Law Enforcement Officers	57.7
	Law Enforcement Officers Offset	49.5

	Category	Cost Factor (%)
Federal Employees Retirement System (FERS)	Regular Employees	14.8
	Regular Employees - Revised Annuity Employees (RAE)	15.4
	Regular Employees - Further Revised Annuity Employees (FRAE)	15.5
	Law Enforcement Officers	32.8
	Law Enforcement Officers Offset - RAE	33.5
	Law Enforcement Officers Offset - FRAE	33.6

The cost to be paid by other agencies is the total calculated future costs, less employee and employer contributions. In addition, other retirement benefits, which include health and life insurance that are paid by other federal entities, must also be recorded.

Imputed Intra-Departmental Financing Sources as defined in SFFAS No. 4, *Managerial Cost Accounting Concepts and Standards for the Federal Government,* are the unreimbursed portion of the full costs of goods and services received by the FBI from a providing entity that is part of the DOJ. Recognition is required for those transactions determined to be material to the receiving entity. The determination of whether the cost is material requires considerable judgment based on the specific facts and circumstances of each type of good or service provided. SFFAS No. 4 also states that costs for broad and general support need not be recognized by the receiving entity, unless such services form a vital and integral part of the operations or output of the receiving entity. Costs are considered broad and general if they are provided to many, if not all, reporting components and not specifically related to the receiving entity's output. The FBI does not have any imputed intra-departmental financing sources.

For the Fiscal Years Ended September 30, 2015 and 2014

	2015	2014
Imputed Inter-Departmental Financing		
Treasury Judgment Fund	$ 5,988	$ 3,151
Health Insurance	162,366	155,306
Life Insurance	704	699
Pension	88,638	135,488
Total Imputed Financing	$ 257,696	$ 294,644

18.   Information Related to the Statement of Budgetary Resources

Apportionment Categories of Obligations Incurred:

The apportionment categories are determined in accordance with the guidance provided in Part 4, *Instructions on Budget Execution*, of OMB Circular A-11, *Preparation, Submission and Execution of the Budget*. Category A represents resources apportioned for calendar quarters. Category B spending includes funds appropriated for digital technology upgrades and construction funding for projects, such as: the FBI's Secure Work Environment Program, Biometrics Technology Center, Terrorist Explosive Device Analytic Center, Hazardous Devices School, DOJ Consolidated Data Center, and the training academy facility at Quantico, Virginia. Category B also includes mortgage fraud investigations, operations along the U.S. southwest border, Department of State funding, Hurricane Sandy supplemental, Law Enforcement Wireless Communication funding, and Spectrum AWS Funding.

	Direct Obligations Incurred	Reimbursable Obligations Incurred	Total Obligations Incurred
For the Fiscal Year Ended September 30, 2015			
Obligations Apportioned Under:			
Category A	$ 8,448,471	$ 1,085,274	$ 9,533,745
Category B	165,197	5,542	170,739
Total	$ 8,613,668	$ 1,090,816	$ 9,704,484
For the Fiscal Year Ended September 30, 2014			
Obligations Apportioned Under:			
Category A	$ 8,179,605	$ 1,103,553	$ 9,283,158
Category B	196,181	7,389	203,570
Total	$ 8,375,786	$ 1,110,942	$ 9,486,728

Status of Undelivered Orders:

Undelivered Orders (UDO) represent the amount of goods and/or services ordered, which have not been actually or constructively received. This amount includes any orders which may have been prepaid or advanced but for which delivery or performance has not yet occurred.

As of September 30, 2015 and 2014	2015	2014
UDO Obligations Unpaid	$ 2,125,064	$ 2,179,546
UDO Obligations Prepaid/Advanced	74,125	26,343
Total UDO	$ 2,199,189	$ 2,205,889

18.   Information Related to the Statement of Budgetary Resources (continued)

Legal Arrangements Affecting Use of Unobligated Balances:

Unobligated balances represent the cumulative amount of budget authority that is not obligated and that remains available for obligation based on annual legislative requirements and other enabling authorities, unless otherwise restricted. The use of unobligated balances is restricted based on annual legislation requirements and other enabling authorities. Funds are appropriated on an annual, multi-year, and no-year basis. Appropriated funds shall expire on the last day of availability and are no longer available for new obligations. Unobligated balances in unexpired fund symbols are available in the next fiscal year for new obligations unless some restrictions have been placed on those funds by law. Amounts in expired fund symbols are not available for new obligations, but may be used to adjust previously established obligations.

Statement of Budgetary Resources vs. the Budget of the United States Government:

The Statement of Budgetary Resources versus the Budget of the U.S. Government as of September 30, 2014 is presented below.

The reconciliation as of September 30, 2015 is not presented because the submission of the Budget of the United States Government (Budget) for FY 2017, which presents the execution of the FY 2015 Budget, occurs after publication of these financial statements. The DOJ Budget Appendix can be found on the OMB website (http://www.whitehouse.gov/omb/budget) and will be available in early February 2016.

Expired Funds and Offsetting Receipts are reported in the FBI's Statement of Budgetary Resources, but not reported in the Budget. The principal component of the amounts presented on the Other line are attributed to rounding.

For the Fiscal Year Ended September 30, 2014 (Dollars in Millions)	Budgetary Resources	Obligations Incurred	Distributed Offsetting Receipts	Net Outlays
Statement of Budgetary Resources (SBR)	$ 10,808	$ 9,487	$ 3	$ 7,738
Funds not Reported in the Budget				
Expired Funds	(294)	(83)	-	-
Offsetting Receipts	-	-	(3)	2
Other	1	-	-	-
Budget of the United States Government	$ 10,515	$ 9,404	$ -	$ 7,740

19.   Net Custodial Revenue Activity

For the fiscal years ended September 30, 2015 and 2014, the FBI collected $5,214 and $5,405, respectively, in restitution payments, seized abandoned cash, and project generated proceeds. These collections were incidental to the FBI's mission. Since the FBI does not have statutory authority to use these funds, the FBI remits these funds upon receipt to the U.S. Treasury's General Fund. As of September 30, 2015 and 2014, the FBI had custodial liabilities of $19 and $0, respectively.

20. Reconciliation of Net Cost of Operations to Budget

For the Fiscal Years Ended September 30, 2015 and 2014

	2015	2014
Resources Used to Finance Activities		
Budgetary Resources Obligated		
Obligations Incurred	$ 9,704,484	$ 9,486,728
Less: Spending Authority from Offsetting Collections and Recoveries	1,430,438	1,376,603
Obligations Net of Offsetting Collections and Recoveries	8,274,046	8,110,125
Less: Offsetting Receipts	(1,153)	3,360
Net Obligations	8,275,199	8,106,765
Other Resources		
Transfers-In/Out Without Reimbursement	25,800	112,458
Imputed Financing from Costs Absorbed by Others (Note 17)	257,696	294,644
Other	(10,836)	(8,193)
Net Other Resources Used to Finance Activities	272,660	398,909
Total Resources Used to Finance Activities	8,547,859	8,505,674
Resources Used to Finance Items not Part of the Net Cost of Operations		
Net Change in Budgetary Resources Obligated for Goods, Services, and Benefits Ordered but not Yet Provided	13,376	(408,499)
Resources That Fund Expenses Recognized in Prior Periods (Note 21)	(15,295)	(3,117)
Budgetary Offsetting Collections and Receipts That do not Affect Net Cost of Operations	(1,140)	3,385
Resources That Finance the Acquisition of Assets	(399,116)	(438,460)
Other Resources or Adjustments to Net Obligated Resources That do not Affect Net Cost of Operations	7,111	(3,371)
Total Resources Used to Finance Items not Part of the Net Cost of Operations	(395,064)	(850,062)
Total Resources Used to Finance the Net Cost of Operations	$ 8,152,795	$ 7,655,612
Components That Will Require or Generate Resources in Future Periods (Note 21)	$ 16,972	$ 5,814
Depreciation and Amortization	477,671	344,961
Revaluation of Assets or Liabilities	25,754	12,642
Other	(10,739)	(68,952)
Total Components of Net Cost of Operations That Will not Require or Generate Resources in the Current Period	509,658	294,465
Net Cost of Operations	$ 8,662,453	$ 7,950,077

Federal Bureau of Investigation   59

These notes are an integral part of the financial statements.

21. Explanation of Differences Between Liabilities not Covered by Budgetary Resources and Components of Net Cost of Operations Requiring or Generating Resources in Future Periods

Liabilities that are not covered by realized budgetary resources and for which there is no certainty that budgetary authority will be realized, such as the enactment of an appropriation, are considered liabilities not covered by budgetary resources. These liabilities totaling $525,932 and $526,144 as of September 30, 2015 and 2014, respectively, are discussed in Note 10, Liabilities not Covered by Budgetary Resources. Decreases in these liabilities result from current year budgetary resources that were used to fund expenses recognized in prior periods. Increases in these liabilities represent unfunded expenses that were recognized in the current period. These increases along with the change in the portion of exchange revenue receivables from the public, which are not considered budgetary resources until collected, represent components of current period net cost of operations that will require or generate budgetary resources in future periods. The changes in liabilities not covered by budgetary resources and receivables generating resources in future periods are comprised of the following:

For the Fiscal Years Ended September 30, 2015 and 2014

	2015	2014
Resources that Fund Expenses Recognized in Prior Periods		
Decrease in Liabilities Not Covered by Budgetary Resources:		
Decrease in Accrued Annual and Compensatory Leave Liabilities	$ -	$ (3,117)
Decrease in Actuarial FECA Liabilities	(6,949)	-
Decrease in Contingent Liabilties	(8,283)	-
Decrease in Other Unfunded Employment Related Liabilities	(63)	-
Total Decrease in Liabilities Not Covered by Budgetary Resources	(15,295)	(3,117)
Total Resources that Fund Expenses Recognized in Prior Periods	$ (15,295)	$ (3,117)
Components That Will Require or Generate Resources in Future Periods		
(Increase)/Decrease in Exchange Revenue Receivable from the Public	$ (1,652)	$ 923
(Increase)/Decrease in Surcharge Revenue Receivable from Other Federal Agencies	3,541	(9,474)
Increase in Liabilities Not Covered by Budgetary Resources:		
Increase in Accrued Annual and Compensatory Leave Liabilities	13,858	-
Increase in Actuarial FECA Liabilities	-	9,154
Increase in Accrued FECA Liabilities	495	1,524
Increase in Contingent Liabilities	-	2,727
Increase in Other Unfunded Employment Related Liabilities	-	4
Increase in Environmental and Disposal Liabilities	730	956
Total Increase in Liabilities Not Covered by Budgetary Resources	15,083	14,365
Total Components That Will Require or Generate Resources in Future Periods	$ 16,972	$ 5,814

U.S. DEPARTMENT OF JUSTICE

FEDERAL BUREAU OF INVESTIGATION

REQUIRED SUPPLEMENTARY INFORMATION
(UNAUDITED)

U.S. Department of Justice
Federal Bureau of Investigation
Combining Statement of Budgetary Resources
By Major Appropriation
For the Fiscal Year Ended September 30, 2015

Dollars in Thousands		CNST		S&E		2015 TOTAL
Budgetary Resources:						
Unobligated Balance, Brought Forward, October 1	$	66,159	$	1,255,083	$	1,321,242
Recoveries of Prior Year Unpaid Obligations		10,694		214,841		225,535
Other Changes in Unobligated Balances		-		(39,791)		(39,791)
Unobligated Balance from Prior Year Budget Authority, Net		76,853		1,430,133		1,506,986
Appropriations (discretionary and mandatory)		115,000		8,874,686		8,989,686
Spending Authority from Offsetting Collections (discretionary and mandatory)		1,666		1,203,237		1,204,903
Total Budgetary Resources	**$**	**193,519**	**$**	**11,508,056**	**$11,701,575**
Status of Budgetary Resources:						
Obligations Incurred	$	114,584	$	9,589,900	$	9,704,484
Unobligated Balance, End of Year:						
Apportioned		78,837		1,530,850		1,609,687
Unapportioned		98		387,306		387,404
Total Unobligated Balance - End of Year		78,935		1,918,156		1,997,091
Total Status of Budgetary Resources	**$**	**193,519**	**$**	**11,508,056**	**$11,701,575**
Change in Obligated Balance:						
Unpaid Obligations:						
Unpaid Obligations, Brought Forward, October 1	$	252,672	$	2,531,168	$	2,783,840
Obligations Incurred		114,584		9,589,900		9,704,484
Outlays, Gross		(115,893)		(9,311,209)		(9,427,102)
Recoveries of Prior Year Unpaid Obligations		(10,694)		(214,841)		(225,535)
Unpaid Obligations, End of Year		240,669		2,595,018		2,835,687
Uncollected Payments:						
Uncollected Payments from Federal Sources, Brought Forward, October 1		-		(606,615)		(606,615)
Change in Uncollected Customer Payments from Federal Sources		-		69,389		69,389
Uncollected Customer Payments from Federal Sources, End of Year		-		(537,226)		(537,226)
Memorandum (non-add) Entries:						
Obligated Balance, Start of Year	$	252,672	$	1,924,553	$	2,177,225
Obligated Balance, End of Year	$	240,669	$	2,057,792	$	2,298,461
Budgetary Authority and Outlays, Net:						
Budgetary Authority, Gross (discretionary and mandatory)	$	116,666	$	10,077,923	$	10,194,589
Less: Actual Offsetting Collections (discretionary and mandatory)		1,666		1,272,626		1,274,292
Change in Uncollected Customer Payments from Federal Sources (discretionary and mandatory)		-		69,389		69,389
Budgetary Authority, Net (discretionary and mandatory)	**$**	**115,000**	**$**	**8,874,686**	**$ 8,989,686**
Outlays, Gross (discretionary and mandatory)	$	115,893	$	9,311,209	$	9,427,102
Less: Actual Offsetting Collections (discretionary and mandatory)		1,666		1,272,626		1,274,292
Outlays, Net (discretionary and mandatory)		114,227		8,038,583		8,152,810
Less: Distributed Offsetting Receipts		-		(1,153)		(1,153)
Agency Outlays, Net (discretionary and mandatory)	**$**	**114,227**	**$**	**8,039,736**	**$ 8,153,963**

Dollars in Thousands		CNST		S&E		2014 TOTAL
Budgetary Resources:						
Unobligated Balance, Brought Forward, October 1	$	76,565	$	1,047,874	$	1,124,439
Recoveries of Prior Year Unpaid Obligations		7,712		190,018		197,730
Other Changes in Unobligated Balances		-		(38,515)		(38,515)
Unobligated Balance from Prior Year Budget Authority, Net		84,277		1,199,377		1,283,654
Appropriations (discretionary and mandatory)		97,482		8,247,961		8,345,443
Spending Authority from Offsetting Collections (discretionary and mandatory)		4,184		1,174,689		1,178,873
Total Budgetary Resources	$	**185,943**	$	**10,622,027**	$	**10,807,970**
Status of Budgetary Resources:						
Obligations Incurred	$	119,784	$	9,366,944	$	9,486,728
Unobligated Balance, End of Period:						
Apportioned		66,157		1,043,875		1,110,032
Unapportioned		2		211,208		211,210
Total Unobligated Balance - End of Year		66,159		1,255,083		1,321,242
Total Status of Budgetary Resources	$	**185,943**	$	**10,622,027**	$	**10,807,970**
Change in Obligated Balance:						
Unpaid Obligations:						
Unpaid Obligations, Brought Forward, October 1	$	279,003	$	2,146,791	$	2,425,794
Obligations Incurred		119,784		9,366,944		9,486,728
Outlays, Gross		(138,403)		(8,792,549)		(8,930,952)
Recoveries of Prior Year Unpaid Obligations		(7,712)		(190,018)		(197,730)
Unpaid Obligations, End of Year		252,672		2,531,168		2,783,840
Uncollected Payments:						
Uncollected Payments from Federal Sources, Brought Forward, October 1		-		(617,526)		(617,526)
Change in Uncollected Customer Payments from Federal Sources		-		10,911		10,911
Uncollected Customer Payments from Federal Sources		-		(606,615)		(606,615)
Memorandum (non-add) Entries:						
Obligated Balance, Start of Year	$	**279,003**	$	**1,529,265**	$	**1,808,268**
Obligated Balance, End of Year	$	**252,672**	$	**1,924,553**	$	**2,177,225**
Budgetary Authority and Outlays, Net:						
Budgetary Authority, Gross (discretionary and mandatory)	$	101,666	$	9,422,650	$	9,524,316
Less: Actual Offsetting Collections (discretionary and mandatory)		4,184		1,185,600		1,189,784
Change in Uncollected Customer Payments from Federal Sources (discretionary and mandatory)		-		10,911		10,911
Budgetary Authority, Net (discretionary and mandatory)	$	**97,482**	$	**8,247,961**	$	**8,345,443**
Outlays, Gross (discretionary and mandatory)	$	138,403	$	8,792,549	$	8,930,952
Less: Actual Offsetting Collections (discretionary and mandatory)		4,184		1,185,600		1,189,784
Outlays, Net (discretionary and mandatory)		134,219		7,606,949		7,741,168
Less: Distributed Offsetting Receipts		-		3,360		3,360
Agency Outlays, Net (discretionary and mandatory)	$	**134,219**	$	**7,603,589**	$	**7,737,808**

This page intentionally left blank.

U.S. DEPARTMENT OF JUSTICE

FEDERAL BUREAU OF INVESTIGATION

OTHER INFORMATION
(UNAUDITED)

This page intentionally left blank.

U.S. Department of Justice
Federal Bureau of Investigation
Combined Schedules of Spending
For the Fiscal Years Ended September 30, 2015 and 2014

Dollars in Thousands		2015		2014
What Money is Available to Spend?				
Total Resources	$	11,701,575	$	10,807,970
Less Amount Available but Not Agreed to be Spent		1,609,687		1,110,032
Less Amount Not Available to be Spent		387,404		211,210
Total Amounts Agreed to be Spent	**$**	**9,704,484**	**$**	**9,486,728**
How was the Money Spent?				
Personnel Compensation and Benefits				
1100　Personnel Compensation	$	3,655,324	$	3,520,180
1200　Personnel Benefits		1,466,436		1,468,061
1300　Former Personnel		3,559		14,016
Other Program Related Expenses				
2100　Travel and Transportation of Persons		209,766		167,395
2200　Transportation of Things		22,450		14,319
2300　Rent, Communications, and Utilities		1,011,860		1,066,053
2400　Printing and Reproduction		1,744		3,615
2500　Other Contractual Services		2,575,498		2,303,156
2600　Supplies and Materials		164,000		165,794
3100　Equipment		490,426		677,934
3200　Land and Structures		100,719		82,857
4100　Grants, Subsidies, and Contributions		-		300
4200　Insurance Claims and Indemnities		2,702		3,048
Total Amounts Agreed to be Spent	**$**	**9,704,484**	**$**	**9,486,728**
Who did the Money go to?				
For Profit	$	2,617,191	$	2,515,424
Government		2,624,797		2,505,574
Employees		3,655,324		3,520,180
Grants		-		300
Other		807,172		945,250
Total Amounts Agreed to be Spent	**$**	**9,704,484**	**$**	**9,486,728**